THE GREENH,

Literary Companion

TO AMERICAN LITERATURE

READINGS ON

ETHAN FROME

Christopher Smith, *Book Editor*

David L. Bender, *Publisher*
Bruno Leone, *Executive Editor*
Bonnie Szumski, *Series Editor*

Greenhaven Press, Inc., San Diego, CA

Every effort has been made to trace the owners of copyrighted material. The articles in this volume may have been edited for content, length, and/or reading level. The titles have been changed to enhance the editorial purpose. Those interested in locating the original source will find the complete citation on the first page of each article.

Library of Congress Cataloging-in-Publication Data

Readings on Ethan Frome / Christopher Smith, book editor.
    p.   cm. — (The Greenhaven Press literary companion to American literature)
    Includes bibliographical references (p.   ) and index.
    ISBN 0-7377-0199-4 (lib. bdg. : alk. paper). —
ISBN 0-7377-0198-6 (pbk. : alk. paper)
    1. Wharton, Edith, 1862–1937. Ethan Frome. I. Smith, Christopher. II. Series.
PS3545.H16 E736   2000
813'.52—dc21   99-047624

Cover photo: Archive Photos

In those days the snowbound villages of New England were still grim places, morally and physically: insanity, incest and slow mental and moral starvation were hidden away behind the paintless wooden house-fronts of the long village street, or in the isolated farm houses on the neighbouring hills.

—*Edith Wharton on* Ethan Frome,
from A Backward Glance *(1934)*

Contents

Chapter 1: The Sources and Setting of *Ethan Frome*

Chapter 2: Style, Technique, and Theme in *Ethan Frome*

Chapter 4: The Case for and Against *Ethan Frome*

FOREWORD

The story's bare facts are simple: The captain, an old and
scarred seafarer, walks with a peg leg made of whale ivory.
He relentlessly drives his crew to hunt the world's oceans for
the great white whale that crippled him. After a long search,
the ship encounters the whale and a fierce battle ensues. Finally the captain drives his harpoon into the whale, but the
harpoon line catches the captain about the neck and drags
him to his death.

A simple story, a straightforward plot—yet, since the 1851
publication of Herman Melville's *Moby-Dick*, readers and
critics have found many meanings in the struggle between
Captain Ahab and the whale. To some, the novel is a cau-
tionary tale that depicts how Ahab's obsession with revenge
leads to his insanity and death. Others believe that the whale
represents the unknowable secrets of the universe and that
Ahab is a tragic hero who dares to challenge fate by attempting to discover this knowledge. Perhaps Melville intended
Ahab as a criticism of Americans' tendency to become involved in well-intentioned but irrational causes. Or did Melville model Ahab after himself, letting his fictional character
express his anger at what he perceived as a cruel and distant
god?

Although literary critics disagree over the meaning of
Moby-Dick, readers do not need to choose one particular interpretation in order to gain an understanding of Melville's

novel. Instead, by examining various analyses, they can gain numerous insights into the issues that lie under the surface of the basic plot. Studying the writings of literary critics can also aid readers in making their own assessments of *Moby-Dick* and other literary works and in developing analytical thinking skills.

The Greenhaven Literary Companion Series was created with these goals in mind. Designed for young adults, this unique anthology series provides an engaging and comprehensive introduction to literary analysis and criticism. The essays included in the Literary Companion Series are chosen for their accessibility to a young adult audience and are expertly edited in consideration of both the reading and comprehension levels of this audience. In addition, each essay is introduced by a concise summation that presents the contributing writer's main themes and insights. Every anthology in the Literary Companion Series contains a varied selection of critical essays that cover a wide time span and express diverse views. Wherever possible, primary sources are represented through excerpts from authors' notebooks, letters, and journals and through contemporary criticism.

Each title in the Literary Companion Series pays careful consideration to the historical context of the particular author or literary work. In-depth biographies and detailed chronologies reveal important aspects of authors' lives and emphasize the historical events and social milieu that influenced their writings. To facilitate further research, every anthology includes primary and secondary source bibliographies of articles and/or books selected for their suitability for young adults. These engaging features make the Greenhaven Literary Companion series ideal for introducing students to literary analysis in the classroom or as a library resource for young adults researching the world's great authors and literature.

Exceptional in its focus on young adults, the Greenhaven Literary Companion Series strives to present literary criticism in a compelling and accessible format. Every title in the series is intended to spark readers' interest in leading American and world authors, to help them broaden their understanding of literature, and to encourage them to formulate their own analyses of the literary works that they read. It is the editors' hope that young adult readers will find these anthologies to be true companions in their study of literature.

INTRODUCTION

When *Ethan Frome* was published in 1911, the reviews were mixed and Edith Wharton expressed disappointment in the novel's respectable but somewhat sluggish sales. Since that time though, *Ethan Frome* has become Wharton's best-known, most widely read novel, and it has been translated into many different languages. For a long time after her death, it was the work for which she was most remembered, and the novel's continued popularity led to its adaptation as a successful film in 1993, starring Liam Neeson in the role of Ethan. With its masterful creation of character relationships and the artistry with which Wharton relates her tale, both readers and writers alike can gain a great deal from reading this short but densely detailed novel.

Part of *Ethan Frome*'s appeal lies in its unsparing glimpse into small-town New England life in the late nineteenth century. Wharton lived in the New England countryside and came to have an insightful understanding of its inhabitants. Her knowledge of the region's historical and religious roots also finds its way into the shape and texture of *Ethan Frome*. This regional emphasis explores universal themes, however. Wharton knew that the passions that rule men's and women's lives, and the sources of human frustration and unhappiness, are the same no matter where they live. Therefore, one cannot help but be affected by Ethan's barely articulated desires and yearnings, Mattie Silver's vital, magnetic appeal, and Zeena's mean-spirited, sickly neurosis. How these individuals struggle among themselves, who triumphs, and why Wharton allows cruelty to prevail over potential good, offers a profound investigation into what it is that motivates and sometimes destroys individuals.

Aside from its masterful portrayal of human desires and conflicts, the novel's craft—the care and skill that went into its construction—rewards a close reading and offers an outstanding example of how technique can enhance content.

Wharton would later say that, while writing *Ethan Frome*, she had for the first time as a writer felt completely in control of her material, and there is no doubt that the novel illustrates her artistry at the height of its powers. The novel brings together many genres: its persistent realism, Gothic elements, and the pessimistic inevitability of a Naturalist novel are effortlessly incorporated into the setting and plot. At a deeper level, the text utilizes a sophisticated network of images and symbols that strengthen and give credibility to the novel's characters and their conflicts. Underlying the density of *Ethan Frome*'s imagery and symbolism are themes common to all great literature: the destructive power of repression, the sense of shame that overshadows so many human actions, and the terrible cost exacted by both love and hate.

Readings on Ethan Frome introduces a range of responses to the novel written by some of the most respected critics of Wharton's work from the last fifty years. The volume is divided into four chapters, each of which focuses on particular aspects of *Ethan Frome*'s form and content. Essays on such traditional features as the novel's symbolism, setting, and thematic richness are balanced by feminist explorations of the characters and debates over whether the novel as a whole is a success. Despite the variety of their focus, all of the selections illustrate the richness of, as well as the continuing interest in, this masterpiece of thwarted love and its consequences.

EDITH WHARTON: A BIOGRAPHY

At the time of her death in 1937, Edith Wharton was one of the most loved, most successful American writers of the twentieth century. Wharton's novels, short stories, travel sketches, and essay collections (on topics as varied as war, architecture, and gardening) offer a glimpse of a world that has long since vanished. Yet the changes she lived through were profound and far-reaching. Consider, for instance, that she was born near the beginning of the American Civil War. Abraham Lincoln was president of the United States, and the continued existence of the nation was in serious jeopardy. On the other side of the Atlantic, Queen Victoria presided over a powerful British empire so huge that the sun never set on it. In Edith Wharton's lifetime, civilization had to adapt itself to inventions such as electricity, moving pictures, automobiles, and planes—to name just a few. Edith Wharton saw the grandeur of late–nineteenth-century European civilization shattered by World War I; at the time of her death, Europe stood poised on the verge of another world war that would once again destroy Europe. In Edith Wharton's lifetime, the American nation had been transformed from a collection of divergent and mutually hostile states into the world's most powerful nation. Wharton biographer R.W.B. Lewis is quite correct in his assertion that the "various tides of history flowed over the years of Edith Wharton's life."

Along with the political and historical changes that characterized Wharton's years were those that impacted literature, the aspect of her life for which she is remembered. Her first poems were published at the insistence of Henry Wadsworth Longfellow, an American poet born in 1807, whose moral musings on nature and humankind seem quaint and irrelevant when we read them today. By the 1930s, she shared the world literary stage with "modernist" writers such as F. Scott Fitzgerald, T.S. Eliot, James Joyce, and Ernest Hemingway. The kinds of immense changes Wharton lived through are richly documented in her writing. She understood very well the often repressed and thwarted desires of all human beings, as well as how often people sacrifice happiness for security. Wharton also predated the modern feminist movement in the way she wrote so perceptively on the kinds of obstacles confronting women as they strove to fulfill their potential. To read her work and know about her life is to be taken back into a time and place remote from our own experience; however, one is also struck by how closely she communicates the dilemmas and hard choices that are part of our lives today.

A LIFE OF WEALTH AND PRIVILEGE

Edith Newbold Jones was born on January 24, 1862, into a life and society of immense wealth and privilege that very few people ever know. Her family could trace its origins back to the Puritan settlements of the 1630s, and her mother's grandfather, Ebenezer Stevens, performed with distinction during the Revolutionary War. In 1773 he was part of the group of men responsible for dumping British tea into Boston harbor, and he later fought beside and became a close friend of the French hero of the Revolution, Lafayette. After the Revolutionary War, Stevens had a successful life in both the commercial and political worlds. He eventually owned a fleet of trading ships, became an agent of the War Department, and was elected to the New York assembly. His children married into prestigious New York families, which assured the ongoing success and extensive connections of the Stevens clan. The families of Edith's mother and father (her parents married in 1844) both had, by the time Edith was born, accumulated vast amounts of land and real estate in New York City. These assets would continue to appreciate in value, and the income from them allowed the Jones family to travel widely, live luxuriously, and entertain lavishly.

In 1852 novelist Herman Melville wrote that, in American cities, "families rise and burst like bubbles in a vat." By this, he meant that nineteenth-century America was characterized by rapid change and fluctuating fortunes. Wealth was often made or lost overnight, and newly wealthy families sought entry into what was deemed polite, genteel "society." This so-called society was, in turn, just as determined to keep them out. The New York world Edith Jones was born into comprised a rather exclusive set of families fiercely protective of their status and hostile to newcomers. These families wanted to preserve a sense of "old money" aristocracy—a world of continuity, good taste, and stability—as opposed to an emerging class of enormously wealthy industrialists whose ostentatious, vulgar display of "new money" was seen as utterly appalling. The key to membership in this exclusive aristocracy was in being able to trace your lineage back through generations—the more the better. One had to have blood ties with other families of similar wealth, taste, and background. What resulted was a kind of small "tribe" that held onto its rituals and traditions in the midst of a rapidly growing, changing New York City. Everyone in Edith's circle knew where everyone else came from, and they all protected each other from social "intruders" who did not have the extensive ties necessary to be able to attend the dances, operas, and dinner parties that constituted "old society" life. This society came to be known as "the 400," because that was the number of people who could fit into socialite Caroline Astor's ballroom, and only the very best, very oldest families would ever be asked. While this society enjoyed a spectacular heyday in the 1870s and 1880s, by the end of the century its fortifications had been breached by the extraordinary wealth of the new post–Civil War industrial "robber barons." It appears that wealth had the final say over brilliant manners and polite conversation, and Edith's New York novels—*The House of Mirth, The Custom of the Country,* and *The Age of Innocence* —brilliantly document this social struggle.

Edith could at an early age have settled into this very comfortable and well-ordered society without ever questioning its values and assumptions, and she could have lived a thoroughly pampered, privileged, and unremarkable life. As a young woman, it was expected that she would become accomplished in and would master the complex social web of dinner parties, music, dancing, and the ritualistic display of wealth, taste, and manners. A woman was expected to marry early, wisely, and well, and then bear children who would be coddled and governessed all through their early years, as Edith herself had been. It was a seductive but severely limited way of life, and Edith would come to notice this society's understated yet powerful hostility toward anyone (especially women) who sought to lead a more intellectual, questioning life. Added to the circumscribed role women were forced into playing was the fact that this fiercely protective "tribe," with its complex set of rules and rituals, demanded absolute conformity. It is therefore not surprising that some of Edith

Wharton's best fiction revisits this remarkable but slowly vanishing society. Within this setting, she ruthlessly explores not only what the society she knew did to women but also the damage it inflicted on the desires and aspirations of those who sought to expand their horizons beyond its confines.

SIX YEARS IN EUROPE

The Jones's income, which enabled them to live in such luxury, came mainly from properties they owned in New York City. With the decline in land values and rent income immediately following the Civil War, Edith's father, George Frederic Jones, decided to relocate to Europe, which at that time was a cheaper place to live than New York City. Both of Edith's parents had fond memories of Europe, where they had lived and traveled after they had married. The family's move initiated Edith's experience of and life-long love affair with Europe. While her brother Freddy (who was sixteen years her senior and to whom she was never close) studied law at Cambridge, the family traveled through England, Italy, and Spain before finally settling in Paris. During a visit to Germany in 1870, Edith nearly died of typhoid fever. But otherwise she would remember the family's extended stay in Europe as a happy, idyllic time. Europe was now, as she would later say, in her blood, and by the time the family returned to America in 1872, she could speak French, Italian, and German. In Europe, Edith had also become a voracious reader of European literature, and she had been exposed to the architectural wonders of Gothic cathedrals, Renaissance palaces, and the artistry of landscape gardening. These aspects of European culture would stay with her for the rest of her life, whether she made her home in America or France. Her novels and short stories also share the fascination that her close friend, novelist Henry James, had with how Americans either succeeded or failed to adapt to the mysteries and splendors of Europe.

THE BEGINNING OF A WRITING CAREER

Upon their return, the Jones family settled into a comfortable home in a fashionable part of New York City, and Edith's education in the sheltered, exclusive social events and rituals of Old New York truly began. While she was given lessons by private tutors, her most serious education was self-directed and took place in her father's well-stocked library. There, she read deeply and intensively the masterpieces of Western literature—from Homer and Dante to Shakespeare and the English romantic poets. She later said that these afternoons in her father's library offered her "a secret ecstasy of communion"—an escape from what she already saw as the placid, anti-intellectual mediocrity of her social circle. Already Edith was finding the life for which she was being groomed claustrophobic, and already literature was becoming a means by which she could assert her independence from it. Edith's reading life, therefore, remained a passion she did not readily share with others, but it soon translated into a desire to write. At the age of twelve, she ambitiously began and completed her first novel, *Fast and Loose*. While it bears all the hallmarks of a work written by someone talented yet very young, one can already see the kind of vivid detail and memorable characters that would form such a significant part of her mature novels. Edith also wrote a great deal of poetry, and when she was sixteen, her mother arranged to have a selection of them published under the title *Verses*. Remarkably, and in no small way due to her family's wealth and extensive connections, three of these poems were later published in magazines—the very exclusive *Atlantic Monthly* and *World*. It would, however, be many years before she would publish again.

EDITH'S SOCIAL DEBUT, ROMANTIC ENTANGLEMENTS, AND A DEATH IN THE FAMILY

Edith made her social debut in 1879, meaning that suddenly her life outside of the home expanded beyond going to church and the theater or riding in Central Park with her mother. The spectacle of emerging from under the protective wing of one's family into the intricate whirl of social gatherings, dances, and other assorted entertainments was considered a significant event in the life of a wealthy young woman. Edith remembers the event as agonizing, and it highlights a part of her personality that would stay with her all her life—an often overpowering shyness. Initiation into the "young set" meant socializing with young men and women of the same degree of old money and reliable family connections. A more subtle demand was that of being interested in the same things: social calls and elegant dinner parties, expensive Parisian clothes, and the making and spending of money. While Edith was always clothes- and money-conscious, her favorite topics of conversation—art, literature, and ideas—were beyond most of her companions. What emerged was a quiet, watchful young woman who played by the rules and rituals of her circle; at the same time, Edith was aware of this society's limitations and desired something beyond it.

Since the underlying purpose of a young woman's social debut was to meet and marry a suitable young man, it was not long before Edith met Henry "Harry" Leyden Stevens. Stevens was three years older than Edith and came from what was considered one of those ostentatiously wealthy and socially ambitious "new money" families to which the "old money" was so hostile. The Joneses, along with other well-to-do New York families, passed their summers at Newport, Rhode Island, and at Bar Harbor, Maine, and it was there in 1880 that the courtship began in earnest.

The courtship's progress was, however, interrupted by a pressing family emergency. At fifty-nine years of age, Edith's father's health began to seriously decline, and the family set out for the south of France in the hope that the friendlier climate there might allow him to recuperate. The family settled in Cannes, and Harry Stevens later joined Edith and stayed with her through her father's final illness and death in early 1882. The loss was a blow to Edith. Although she was never close to her mother and had an often difficult and frustrating relationship with her, she had loved her father deeply.

The family returned to Newport for the summer. By August, Edith's engagement to Harry Stevens became official, and the marriage was scheduled for October. However, by the end of October, the marriage had been indefinitely postponed and the engagement broken. While many explanations have been put forward as to why, there seems no doubt that Harry Stevens's mother, a strong-willed and socially powerful woman who had never approved of the match, moved to influence her son against marrying Edith. While it was a painful and embarrassing experience for Edith, she seemed to have reintegrated herself into New York society without too much difficulty, and the next summer she met Walter Berry, a man with whom she would form one of the longest and most important friendships of her life. Berry was from an old and respectable New York family, had attended Harvard, and when he met Edith in 1883, was about to enter the legal profession. Unlike most men in her circle, Berry was not intimidated by Edith's intelligence, and he was a perceptive and discriminating reader of literature. The two spent an intense, happy summer together, and observers fully expected them to become engaged. However, by the end of the summer he left

Bar Harbor, and the couple barely saw each other over the next fourteen years. It appears that Walter Berry had, in modern-day terminology, a commitment problem when it came to women. He remained a bachelor all of his life and was careful to never seriously entangle himself in any sustained relationship. For Edith, the disappointment was far more intensely felt than her broken engagement with Stevens. It is tempting to make connections between a writer's life and her work, and here it is not difficult to equate Edith's early romantic failures with the thwarted romantic hopes and desires of so many of her fictional characters.

MARRIAGE AND THE BEGINNINGS OF A WRITING CAREER

Edith met Edward "Teddy" Wharton the same month that she was disappointed in her hopes of marrying Berry. She and Teddy became engaged in March 1885, and they married in April of the same year. Teddy, a Bostonite, was a friend of Edith's brother Harry and was thirty-three—thirteen years older than Edith—at the time they met. He came from a respectable and financially comfortable family, had spent two undistinguished years at Harvard, and had no intention of pursuing any kind of career. An energetic, amiable man who was happiest when fishing, hunting, or engaged in some other outdoor activity, it seems incredible in hindsight that Edith would have been attracted to, let alone have married, a man such as Teddy. There was never any question that he had any literary or artistic gifts to speak of, and he was no match for Edith intellectually. One can safely speculate that, following the emotional turmoil of her father's death and her failed romances with Stevens and Berry, the stability offered by a superficially likeable suitor such as Teddy was appealing. Added to these considerations was the fact that Edith was guided by the imperatives of a society that saw marriage as the only true goal of a woman. Incredible as it may seem to us now, a woman in the 1880s who was still unmarried at age twenty-three was considered in danger of never marrying at all. A genuine fondness between the two does seem to have sustained their marriage for more than twenty years, yet Edith's biographers agree that, in the words of R.W.B. Lewis, their marriage was characterized by "the virtual—more likely, the total—cessation of their sex life together."

In the late 1880s, the Whartons settled into an undemanding routine of dividing their year between two continents: February through June in Europe (mostly in Italy), and July through January in Newport. If ever there was a time when Edith settled into the undemanding, restrictive life of a wealthy American socialite, it was in these years. She developed a few close friendships in America, but she always felt that another kind of life awaited her in Europe, just as she felt that life in Newport and New York was choking her vast creative potential. Yet 1889 marked something of a turning point for Edith. She inherited a substantial legacy from a distant family relative, and it was enough to guarantee her and Teddy's financial independence and security for the rest of their lives. For some time now, Edith had found the increasingly shallow, pretentious world of Newport insufferable, and the legacy allowed the Whartons to purchase a house in New York City. With this financial independence came a desire to write, which had lain dormant in Edith for a decade. In 1889 and 1890, some four poems and a short story were accepted for publication. The first stirrings of a prolific, professional novelist had begun, but it would be interrupted in 1894 by a severe and prolonged series of "illnesses."

DEPRESSION AND BREAKDOWN

In the summer of 1894, Edith had a nervous breakdown—characterized by nausea, exhaustion, and extreme melancholy—that would more or less incapacitate her for the next two years. The stories and poems from this time deal with frustration and disillusionment in love and marriage, and there is no question that her having to resign herself to a less than satisfactory relationship with Teddy played a significant role in her depression. Added to Edith's domestic situation was the uncertainty surrounding her future. Should she remain something of a society hostess, leading a leisured life in New York and abroad, or should she commit herself fully to her writing? This question was answered in some degree by the respite from her illness and the degree of pleasure she experienced in writing her first book, a collaboration with the architect Ogden Codman titled *The Decoration of Houses* (1897). This work exhibits Edith's expertise in the interior design of upper-class homes, and how to best create a sense of harmony and proportion within each room. Interior design, along with landscape gardening, would remain one of Edith's passions for the rest of her life. In her fiction, the extensive descriptions of houses and gardens often add a great deal to our understanding of the characters that inhabit them and the society that produced them. Edith was assisted in the work's final revisions by Walter Berry, whose presence no doubt helped her emerge from her illness. Edith had not spent any significant amount of time with Berry—now an established attorney and expert in international law—for fourteen years. From this time on, though, he would, along with a small, select group of men and women, form the core of a social and intellectual circle that would sustain her for the rest of her life.

THE EMERGING WRITER

With the exception of a relapse in 1898, Edith had now fully regained her health and began to produce an impressive amount of stories, travel essays, and novels. She was now thirty-seven years old, an age at which many writers have already written their best work; however, she more than compensated for this late start over the next decade. For material, she would draw heavily on her coming of age in New York high society and on her extensive travel through Europe. While she had not written a great deal in the 1880s and 1890s, she had observed and committed to memory people, places, and events that would serve as the foundation for her best work. Her first collection of short stories, *The Greater Inclination*, appeared in 1899. The collection included many of the themes that would be present throughout much of Edith's writing; for example, the most accomplished story, "Souls Belated," examines themes of entrapment in the rigid moral standards of society, the ardent desire to escape this confinement, and the terrible cost any attempted escape exacts. Although it deals with a wealthy man and woman traveling through Europe, the story's themes are not far from the village of Starkfield and the predicament faced by Mattie Silver and Ethan Frome. Already Edith's sharp eye in recording minute yet revealing social details is apparent, as is her irony and unsparing satire of human predicaments and human follies.

The Whartons' life in Newport, New York, and Europe continued into the first years of the 1900s. Edith's extensive travel through Italy bore fruit with the publication of two successful travel books in 1904 and 1905, detailing mostly with her discovery of Italian towns and their art and architecture. Edith's mother died in Paris in June 1901, thus ending any blood ties she had to the generation that preceded her. She and her mother had been anything but close, and Edith's autobiographical writings make clear her disapproval of her mother's rigid, repressed, and withholding character. Often in her fiction, characters whose values are not unlike those of her mother seem to force their will on and dominate the lives of those characters who have larger, more generous natures.

Having finally had enough of Newport and New York, she and Teddy bought a large piece of property near Lenox, Massachusetts, a small resort town in the Berkshire mountains where they had begun to spend their summers. In 1902 the Whartons moved into the Mount, a house she would come to treasure and into which she poured a great deal of her creativity regarding its interior design and the landscaping of the estate's gardens. Over the next seven or eight years, Edith would come to know well the surrounding villages and countryside, and she would use these places and the people who inhabited them in her novellas *Ethan Frome* and *Summer.*

Edith published her first novel, *The Valley of Decision,* in 1902, but it was her second, *The House of Mirth* (1905), that truly established her as a best-selling novelist. *The House of Mirth* drew on the material she knew best: the highest reaches of New York society—detailing its frivolity and irresponsibility as well as its cruelty. The novel also developed for the first time in her work the notion of the outsider (in this case, Lily Bart) who seeks entrance into a materially rich yet morally dubious society that partially accepts but then casually destroys her. *The House of Mirth* sold 140,000 copies in 1905 and established Edith Wharton as a force to be reckoned with in the literary landscape.

Edith Wharton

LIFE IN PARIS AND LENOX

The Valley of Decision had been a historical novel set in eighteenth-century Italy, whereas the far superior *The House of Mirth* had dealth with contemporary America. It was

Henry James, one of the great novelists of the late nineteenth and early twentieth centuries, who had suggested that she write on "the American subject." Edith began correspondence with James in 1900, and her friendship with him was one of the most important of her life. The Whartons would spend some of the happiest times of their lives traveling by car through England and France with James. Edith and James shared a love of literature, art, European culture, and social conversation that made them perfect companions. Along with Walter Berry, James was also Edith's closest adviser in literary matters.

Edith's time in Europe now shifted its focus away from Italy and onto France. From about 1906 until the end of her life, Paris and its immediate environs would form the geographical center of her life. At this time Paris was in the midst of what was known as *la belle epoque*, an era of technological and artistic progress accompanied by an inflexible class system that enabled the wealthy and privileged to live elegant, sumptuous lives. With her wealth and success as a novelist, Edith had privileged access to both the aristocratic and artistic worlds of Paris, and she reveled in both. *La belle epoque* came crashing down with the onset of World War I, but from 1907 to 1914, Edith moved among, and was on equal footing with, some of the most noted social and literary figures of the time.

Summers in Lenox were a more relaxed time, and Edith fell into a routine of writing all morning and entertaining in the afternoons and evenings. In 1907 she had published a novella, *Madame de Treymes*, which developed a theme that would reappear in *Ethan Frome*: a person's entrapment within, and the impossibility of escape from, a disastrous marriage. There is no question that there is an autobiographical impulse behind this theme, and Edith's fiction shows this condition could as easily happen to one born into wealth as it could to a poor New England farmer. Her third novel, *The Fruit of the Tree*, further explores the theme of marital disillusionment and the suffocating confinement that accompanies it. There is no question that in 1906 and 1907, Edith was casting a searching, severe eye on the condition of her marriage. It had long been obvious to her that Teddy was incapable of meeting her emotional and physical needs, and the long yet inevitable process that would culminate in their divorce must have been set in motion at this time.

A LOVE AFFAIR AND DIVORCE

In Paris in April 1906, Edith met Morton Fullerton, an acquaintance of Henry James. Fullerton would visit Lenox in 1907, and it was there that intimations of what would later become a passionate love affair began. Fullerton was an American working in Paris as the correspondent for the London *Times.* He was a talented yet slightly unfocused and idealistic man who seemed to have no difficulty attracting the attention of numerous women. Indeed, Fullerton's affairs and their consequences often consumed a great deal of his time and energy. By the summer of 1908, he and Edith had become lovers.

The ascent of Edith's relationship with Fullerton was accompanied by a serious decline in Teddy Wharton's health. Teddy's ailments seemed similar to Edith's breakdown in the 1890s: nervous depression and various incapacitating physical symptoms that seemed connected to a deep sense of dissatisfaction with the condition of his life. One of Edith's biographers, Shari Benstock, says that Teddy suffered from what we now call manic depression and that it was a trait that ran in the Wharton family. Manic depression is a condition characterized by wild mood swings: between buoyant, energetic joy on the one hand and paralyzing melancholy on the other. Yet for years now, as Edith's literary ambitions and fame rose, and she gathered around her writers, artists, and intellectuals of like-minded interests, Teddy had become increasingly isolated. Jovial and endlessly accommodating, the role he had played for some twenty years in Edith's life was becoming redundant. Furthermore, he could not have been blind to the fact that Edith was beginning to spend an extraordinary amount of time with Morton Fullerton. While Edith and he had been good travel companions, Teddy had gradually been pushed farther and farther out into the margins of Edith's life as her confidence in her own career grew. An avid outdoorsman, he was happiest fishing and hunting in America, while Edith was beginning to see her time in America as an irritating separation from her friends and life in Europe. Added to Teddy's dislike of Parisian life was the fact that, for their entire marriage, Teddy had been entirely dependent financially on Edith's income. While Edith obviously had dissatisfactions arising from their marriage, Teddy had his own grievances, and they no doubt had a catastrophic effect on his mental and physical health.

Throughout 1908 and 1909, Edith and Teddy spent most of

their time apart—he was in America seeking various restorative "cures" for his poor health, and Edith was in Paris with Fullerton. Matters between her and Teddy came to a head in December 1909, when Teddy revealed to Edith that he had embezzled money (about fifty thousand dollars) from her estate for the purpose of his own speculations in the stock market. He also dramatically added that he had purchased an apartment in Boston for his young mistress and an assortment of chorus girls, and he had lived there for most of that year. Although some of what he related to Edith was exaggerated, most of it was true, and it seems that some of his behavior was a kind of rebellion against his financial dependence on Edith and the rapidly diminishing role he was playing in her life.

The affair with Fullerton (which ended in 1910), Teddy's illness, and the disclosure of his behavior in America had a dramatic effect on Edith's writing. From 1908 to 1910, she produced little work of note, other than two rather uneven collections of stories and a travel book on France. The year 1910 was miserable for Edith. Teddy's ill health and neurotic behavior made an attempted reconciliation with him difficult. Divorce was a solution far from Edith's mind since it was still seen as scandalous and was frowned on by the society in which she moved. There was also the fact that, given her affair with Fullerton, she could hardly fault Teddy's adultery without sounding like a hypocrite. Teddy eventually admitted himself into a sanitarium in Switzerland to try and recuperate from his depression and ill health; later, in the hope that a radical change of scenery would help him fully recover, he agreed to take a world tour with a family friend. From 1911 to 1913, there would be attempts at reconciliation, followed by estrangement and bitter accusations, culminating in divorce in April 1913.

A CREATIVE PERIOD IN THE MIDST OF A PERSONAL CRISIS

It was a stressful, unhappy time, yet Teddy's absence, and the need for the escape that fiction writing offered, allowed Edith to begin writing again. In this period she wrote three outstanding works: *The Reef* (1912), *The Custom of the Country* (1913), and the work that initiated this intensely creative spell, *Ethan Frome* (1911).

The work is set in the wretchedly poor and bleak town of (appropriately named) Starkfield, among people whose social and financial circumstances are as far removed from those of Edith Wharton as can be imagined. Yet R.W.B. Lewis has said that the novella is "one of the most autobiographical stories ever written." One can see the accuracy of this comment once a number of autobiographical factors are taken into account. Firstly, there was Teddy's illness and the draining effect it had on Edith. Secondly, there was the intense perception of a more passionate life that she had experienced with Morton Fullerton. Finally, there was the familiar theme of entrapment in a loveless marriage. The novella's ending also illustrates Edith's fear of the catastrophe that arises from any attempt to break free from one's confinement. All these factors are built into the novella: the dominating presence of Zeena's illness, the hopelessly thwarted ambitions Ethan had as a young man and the possibility of renewal he sees in a life with Mattie, and the hatred and sense of mutual recrimination that characterizes the Frome marriage. Of course, the novella ends with the unbearably tragic consequences of Mattie's and Ethan's attempted escape from their circumstances. While Edith's situation was hardly as hopeless as that of Ethan and Mattie, the tone of the work offers a vivid picture of her despair and anxiety over her future at this time. The year 1911, when *Ethan Frome* was written, was the final summer Edith spent in Massachusetts; the Mount was sold in November. With the sale of her beloved estate in Lenox, Edith effectively abandoned America. She would return again only once—in 1923 to receive an honorary doctorate from Yale University.

Following her divorce, Edith traveled widely throughout Europe and North Africa, often in the company of Walter Berry. Biographers have long speculated on whether Berry and Edith were ever lovers, but there is no conclusive evidence to suggest that they were. There is no doubt that, after her affair with Fullerton and her divorce from Teddy, Berry was a constant, central presence in her life until his death in 1927. Ironically, she visited Germany a year before the onset of World War I, an event that would radically change Western civilization and effectively put an end to the genteel, aristocratic world she had known.

THE WAR YEARS IN PARIS

Edith, like almost everyone else in Europe in 1914, thought that the war would be short and glorious, culminating in Britain and France's crushing defeat of Germany and the Austro-Hungarian Empire. Few if any people foresaw the extent to which it would become an agonizing, drawn-out struggle. A month into the war, German troops had swept through Belgium and were within one hundred miles of Paris. At the Battle of the Marne, though, French troops and a small British contingent managed to halt the German advance, and both sides dug in and held their positions. Four years of trench warfare had now begun. Edith's response to these events was remarkable. Rather than fleeing to the safety of England or America, she lived in Paris for virtually the entire war and distinguished herself in her devotion to the French cause.

One of the most pressing problems in the first few months of war was the sheer volume of refugees arriving in Paris from Belgium and the areas of France under attack. Their situation was desperate: they arrived with no money or possessions, no place to stay, nothing to eat, and no prospects of employment. Edith founded and ran the American Hostels for Refugees and displayed a genius for organization in the process. It involved not only finding accommodation for families but also setting up clinics to administer to the refugees' health, supplying clothing, distributing food, and finding employment for them so they could eventually take care of themselves. Later she founded the Children of Flanders Rescue Committee, which not only took in starving refugee children but also offered schooling, work training, and jobs. All of this, of course, took money, and Edith drew heavily on her connections both in Europe and America (as well as her own money) to fund her undertaking. In the first year alone, her organization was responsible for assisting and establishing in Paris nearly ten thousand refugees and their children. As the tide of refugees stabilized at the end of 1915, Edith turned her attention to the immense number of wounded the war was producing, by working to supply the overcrowded hospitals with blankets, clothing, and medical supplies. She often visited the front and wrote articles for publication in America about her experiences there. Infuriated by America's stance of neutrality in the first three years of the war, she wanted to do all she could to commit America by influencing public opinion. These pieces were soon collected into a volume called *Fighting France* (1915), one of her best nonfiction publications.

Many of Wharton's younger French and British friends and acquaintances had enlisted and were killed in the trenches. On the home front, she was hit especially hard by the death of Henry James in February 1916. She would later say that his friendship was "the pride and honor of my life." Edith's perception that the life she had lived and known for over fifty years had come to an end was made plain by the central events in her life at that time: the deaths of a number of her friends in such quick succession, her exhaustion from her refugee work, and the fact that the end of the war was nowhere in sight. While her personal life was characterized by a sense of terrible loss, she was honored for her public achievements. In April 1916 she was made a chevalier of the Legion of Honor, the highest award that a civilian could be given in France (in 1919 she was made chevalier of the Order of Leopold, the Belgian equivalent).

The rest of 1916 was, however, a bleak year. There was talk of Britain negotiating a separate peace with Germany, leaving France to fight on alone, and there were mutinies among French divisions in the trenches. On April 2, 1917, though, the United States, responding to the sinking of its ships by German submarines, declared war on Germany. America's move away from neutrality, which was ultimately decisive in ending the war, shook Edith from out of her depression. Now relieved of many of her duties by organizations such as the Red Cross, she once again turned to her writing. She had published a collection of short stories in 1916, but virtually all of it had been written before the war began. In 1917 she published *Summer*, which she called her "Hot Ethan," since the action takes place in high summer rather than in the dead of winter. The novella is similar to *Ethan Frome* in that it is set in New England and involves frustrated lives and forbidden passion; however, the tale ends on a happier and perhaps more successful note than its New England predecessor. Edith also regained her appetite for travel. Having acquired a taste for North Africa when she visited Algeria and Tunisia before the war, she set out for Morocco toward the end of 1917. She returned to Paris, however, for the last great German offensive—an attempt to win the war before fresh American troops arrived—and lived through long-range artillery attacks on Paris. One shell actually destroyed her first home in Paris at 58 Rue de Varenne but left her current residence—number 53—unscathed.

While Edith shared in the joy the end of the war brought in November 1918, she would write soon after that "these four years have so much changed the whole aspect of life that it is not easy to say now what one's literary tendencies will be when the war is over." Things would indeed never be the same. An entire generation of young men had been all but wiped out. With the triumph of communism in Russia, the crippling of France and Britain due to their war efforts, and the unquestioned dominance America now had over world affairs, a new world order presented itself to the likes of Edith Wharton.

POSTWAR UNCERTAINTY

Edith responded to the radically altered, disconcerting state of society and civilization in a number of ways. Firstly, she created a sense of stability by purchasing and lavishing her attention on two houses in which she would live for the rest of her life: the Pavillon Colombe, twelve miles to the north of Paris, and a winter residence at Hyères in the south of France. Secondly, she gathered around her the remaining circle of friends and made them one of the focal points of her life. Finally, and most importantly for her fiction, she began to reach back into her past life in New York as a source for her novels and stories. Toward the end of her life, Edith wrote her autobiography, *A Backward Glance*—a title that sums up both the nature of her last twenty years and the impetus for her creativity.

The values associated with the nineteenth century truly came to an end in 1914. What lay ahead, and the social conditions that would emerge to replace these values, remained uncertain. In light of the cultural and political vacuum that confronted the world in 1919, it is not surprising that Edith should have returned imaginatively to the nineteenth century, which offered the comfort both of nostalgia and stability. The major works that came out of this retrospective look back and introspective examination of her childhood years— *The Age of Innocence* (1920) and *Old New York* (1924)—came about for another reason, too. Edith's exposure to American culture through the sheer number of Americans in Paris both during and after the war appalled her. She felt that a new kind of American was emerging—money hungry, fundamentally dishonest, and completely ignorant of, or indifferent to, art and culture. In 1920 America had rejected the opportunity of taking on the role of world leader by refusing membership in the League of Nations. This move into what would amount to two decades of isolationism, during which Hitler and Mussolini would lead Europe into another world war, was for Edith the final straw. She saw America's abdication of world leadership and adoptation of an isolationist stance in the world as further proof of America's self-absorbed interest in money-making, and it furthered her disenchantment with her native country.

LITERARY SUCCESS AND HONORS

In light of what Edith saw as the poor state of the modern American, she increasingly saw the 1870s and 1880s New York society as a better, more secure world. While by no means perfect (her fiction would ruthlessly dissect its narrow-mindedness and claustrophobic conformity), fictionally recreating the vanished world of her youth served as a means of harmonizing the solidity of the past and the chaos of the present. It also offered her a means of coming to terms with her past and offered her own life a sense of continuity and purpose.

Although set in 1870s New York, *The Age of Innocence* revisits familiar themes: characters' entrapment in a limited range of possibilities, the desire to escape these choices and secure a more fulfilled life, and the subjugation of a sensitive nature by a narrower, more mean-spirited nature. In Newland Archer, we have a figure much like Ethan Frome. A generous, engaging, yet somewhat weak and indecisive man, Archer is engaged to the vacuous, yet well-connected May Welland. On the eve of his engagement to May, Archer meets and falls in love with the beautiful and charismatic Ellen Olenska, who, having scandalously divorced her dissolute European husband, has returned to New York in the hope of social acceptance. In Countess Olenska, Archer glimpses a kind of life beyond the narrow and rather dull confines of New York society, yet neither he nor Ellen has the courage to decisively act on their respective desires. Meanwhile, May Welland and the society of which she is such a central part, maneuver Archer into submission and ultimate membership in their "tribe." What follows for Archer is a comfortable yet unremarkable existence among the elite of New York society, and Ellen Olenska returns to Europe and lives out her days in Paris. The novel's themes, let alone the familiar pattern of the love triangle, return us again to the world of *Ethan Frome*, even though *The Age of Innocence* is set in the exclusive and visibly wealthy parlors and drawing rooms of Old New York.

The novel was a staggering critical and commercial success for Edith, selling 115,000 copies over the next two years and being successfully adapted for the stage. As a sign of the changing times, she was also paid fifteen thousand dollars for the movie rights to the novel. *The Age of Innocence* was also awarded the Pulitzer Prize in 1921—a crowning achievement in the recognition of Edith Wharton as a major twentieth-century American novelist. With the 1924 publication of *Old New York*, her status as the supreme living practitioner of both the historical novel and the novel of manners reached its peak. She remained one of America's best-selling novelists throughout the 1920s and even during the Great Depression of the 1930s. Yet most critics agree that she reached her creative peak with *The Age of Innocence* and *Old New York*. Novels such as *The Glimpses of the Moon* (1922), *The Mother's Recompense* (1925), and *The Children* (1928) have their brilliant moments, and her novels continued to sell at a tremendous rate. However, many reviewers charged that she had lost touch with the modern world, and the way in which people in the 1920s and 1930s thought and spoke. Given that Edith Wharton's greatest critical and commercial successes came from her brilliant examination of the vanished genteel society of nineteenth-century New York, there is some validity to this criticism.

THE FINAL YEARS

While Edith gained the admiration and friendship of brilliant young writers such as F. Scott Fitzgerald, Sinclair Lewis, and Alberto Moravia, it was the loss of her older, closer friends that characterized her last years. She had first realized this inevitable accompaniment to her own advancing years when Henry James died in 1916, but in 1927 she was devastated by the death of her closest friend, Walter Berry, from a stroke. There is a great deal of controversy over how close Edith and Berry were, but there is no doubt that for forty years he was her intellectual soul mate and closest literary adviser. His absence in her life was one that could not possibly be filled by anyone or anything else. Somewhat ironically, a few months later Edith was informed of Teddy Wharton's death. They had not seen, spoken, or written to each other since their divorce, but these two deaths made her feel that she had reached an age where most of the people with whom she had shared her life's richest years had passed away.

After Berry's death, Edith traveled less but still continued to produce a large amount of novels, short story collections, and nonfiction of uneven quality. While her income fell off somewhat in the wake of the 1929 stock market crash and the depression that followed, she remained one of America's best-selling novelists. She was too wealthy to be financially affected by the economic catastrophe that swept through the United States and Europe, but she was alive to the Depression's political consequences. Edith saw quite clearly the direction Europe was heading with the rise to power of Benito Mussolini in Italy and Adolf Hitler in Germany, and she also saw the extent to which debates about communism would come to dominate the political world. As Europe moved toward another defining conflict, she became even more possessive of her friends and the stability they brought to her life. Wharton's biographer R.W.B. Lewis observes that "More than ever . . . she saw her small circle of friends, devoted to the arts, to beauty, to good conversation and the graces of life, as a last stronghold in a collapsing civilization."

In 1932, at seventy years of age, she began work on her autobiography, *A Backward Glance.* This work turned out to be by far her best work of nonfiction, recreating as it did Old New York and Newport and the grace and splendor of late–nineteenth- and early–twentieth-century Europe. While in many ways it is a withholding performance—many aspects of her personal life would only be uncovered by later biographers—it fully illustrates the extent and intensity of Edith Wharton's involvement in the social and artistic currents of her time. The greatest scenes are those taken from the nineteenth century, and it is not surprising that her last, incomplete novel, *The Buccaneers,* returns again to one of her favorite decades, the 1870s. Thus, in the final years of her life, Edith was recreating her past in fiction and nonfiction. In the process she was attempting to reconstruct her life history both for her reading public and herself.

With the exception of her breakdowns in the 1890s, Edith's physical and mental health had remained robust throughout her life. Although illnesses in 1929 and 1934 had prevented her from going to America to receive an honorary doctorate from Columbia University, Edith managed the rigors of traveling throughout Europe until her death. She recoverd somewhat from a series of strokes in 1937, but they essentially broke her health. Nevertheless, she retained her intellectual vitality into her last days, receiving visitors and writing letters at her home north of Paris. She died on August 11, 1937, and was buried, according to her wishes, near Walter Berry at Versailles.

EDITH WHARTON'S LITERARY REPUTATION

Edith Wharton's popularity and reputation as a writer went into decline in the decade following her death. For a long time she was seen as nothing more than a pale imitation of and lesser talent to her friend Henry James. However, a slow recovery began in the 1950s and 1960s. Critics began to appreciate the understated irony embedded in her novels as well as her mastery of the nuances of individual psychology. Edith Wharton is now celebrated for her ability to incorporate a whole society's rituals, struggles, and beliefs into her novelistic framework. Her creative, independent life and the struggles of her female characters to assert themselves in an oppressive society have drawn intense interest from feminist readers and critics. The publication of two important biographies by noted scholars R.W.B. Lewis and Cynthia Griffin Wolff in 1975 and 1977, respectively, ushered in a boom in Wharton studies that has continued unabated to this day. While *Ethan Frome* has always been widely read, novels such as *The House of Mirth, Summer,* and *The Age of Innocence* have become equally esteemed by readers. Virtually all of her books—novels, short story collections, travel books and essay collections—are still in print. They continue to be read and admired by everyone from literature teachers to moviegoers who, enthralled by movie versions of *Ethan Frome* and *The Age of Innocence,* wish to discover for themselves the writings of this remarkable woman.

PLOT AND CHARACTERS

Ethan Frome begins with a young, educated narrator—an engineer—who is lodging for a winter in Starkfield, Massachusetts. He has been sent there by his employers to work on a nearby power station. While the narrator waits out a carpenter's strike at the power station, he comes to know the town of Starkfield—a small, isolated mountain town—and the hard lives of the people who live there. Starkfield is the kind of town that wears away at the life and vitality of its inhabitants—a town of severely limited choices where, as former stage driver Harmon Gow wryly observes, "Most of the smart ones get away." The narrator is struck in particular by the appearance and tragic demeanor of Ethan Frome, an imposing "ruin of a man." Frome is a daily fixture in the town as he rides in from his ramshackle farm and drags his half-crippled body into the town post office to collect his mail. The narrator then begins to reconstruct the tragic story of Ethan Frome, a story that he hears "bit by bit, from various people, and . . . each time it [is] a different story."

The role of the novel's narrator is important and somewhat controversial. Edith Wharton was confronted with the problem of having to introduce the character of Ethan Frome in the novel's "present" while also having to go back in time to tell what happened to him twenty-four years earlier. She solved this problem by creating a "framing" prologue and epilogue, both of which are told from the narrator's point of view. The rest of the tale goes back in time to the days leading up to Ethan's accident and it is narrated in the third person, with everything being seen through Ethan's eyes. This technique of Wharton's is complicated by her having the narrator present the story of Ethan's past life as an imagined "vision" that becomes clear to him once he enters the Frome household. Wharton later said this was the only way she could think of bringing an uncommunicative character's past together with his present situation. The problem with this technique is that Ethan thinks and feels things the narrator could not possibly know, so it is best to see the novel as being narrated from two different perspectives: by the narrator himself at the beginning and end and by Ethan Frome in the middle.

The narrator hears part of Ethan's story from two townspeople, Harmon Gow and Mrs. Ned Hale. Gow relates details of a sledding accident twenty-four years ago that crippled Ethan back when he was a vigorous twenty-eight-year-old. Gow adds that Ethan was not able to leave Starkfield, like the other "smart ones," because he had to leave school and return home to care for his injured father, his sick mother, and later his wife. Gow sums up Ethan's adult life by observing the role that sickness has played in it: "Sickness and trouble: that's what Ethan's had his plate full up with, ever since the very first helping." Mrs. Hale, obviously moved by the tragedy of Ethan's life, can barely bring herself to talk about him. An unexpected series of events—the severity of the weather and the sudden unavailability of horses at the livery stable—lead to the narrator's reliance on Ethan for daily transport to the train station.

Despite the narrator's efforts to initiate conversation with Ethan, their time together passes mostly in silence. The narrator does, however, find out that Ethan spent some time working in Florida, which gives some indication of the kind of desire to leave Starkfield that possessed Ethan as a young man. The narrator's perception of the lost opportunities that characterize Ethan's life are furthered when Ethan comes upon a book of the narrator's that deals with some recent developments in biochemistry. Once a student of the sciences, Ethan is both curious about the book's content and upset that advances in the field have left him so far behind that he can barely understand it. The narrator feels a growing bond with Ethan, but it is a bond that the mostly silent, emotionally withholding Ethan does not share. One night, after they are caught in a particularly severe snowstorm, the narrator is invited to stay the night at Ethan's farm, where he gathers enough material to fashion an imagined "vision" of Ethan's life story.

The prologue to the novel ends in this way, and the reader is now taken back in time to the days leading up to the sledding accident twenty-four years earlier. Until the epilogue, the novel will be told from Ethan's point of view. Ethan is walking into town from his farm to escort Mattie Silver—a cousin of his wife who is living with the Fromes as a house-keeper—home from a dance. As Wharton lets us into Ethan's thoughts, we quickly learn some background facts regarding Ethan's life. He tried to leave Starkfield and spent a year at a technical college in Worcester, Massachusetts; however, he had to return home after his father was injured in an accident. Remaining in the shadows, he watches Mattie dancing with Dennis Eady, an eligible young bachelor. As she dances with Eady, Ethan's thoughts turn to what Mattie and her living in the Frome house has come to mean to him. Firstly, we see that Mattie is attractive and lively, and a surge of jealousy flows through Ethan when he sees her dancing with another man. Mattie has lived with the Fromes for about a year, and in that time her presence has been for Ethan like "a bit of hopeful young life . . . like the lighting of a fire on a cold hearth." She has awakened in him a sense of life's possibilities, which had lain dormant since he became trapped in Starkfield. It seems to Ethan that she reciprocates the feelings that he has for her, but in his jealousy over her dancing with Dennis Eady, he is somewhat disconcerted. Ethan's feelings are however revived when Mattie refuses a ride home from the dance with Eady, and the conversation Ethan and Mattie have on the way back from town to the farm confirms for the reader their mutual attraction. Two factors cast a shadow over their evolving affection for each other, though. As they talk about how another couple nearly crashed into the elm at the bottom of the town sled run, we have an eerie foreshadowing of their sledding "accident" that will end the novel. There is also a dark foreboding in the fact that Ethan's wife, Zeena, has not been blind to their growing affection for each other. As if to reinforce the presence of Zeena in the lives of both Ethan and Mattie, their intimate conversation is abruptly ended when they arrive at the Frome house and Zeena surprises them by opening the door, looming over them, lantern in hand.

Zeena Frome is seven years older than Ethan and is a hypochondriac, meaning she constantly believes she is ill. Upon being introduced to Zeena, the reader cannot help but see the difference between her sickly, querulous nature and Mattie's warmth and vitality. Yet through her sickliness and the demands it makes on Ethan, we come to see how she controls the Frome household. The next day Ethan learns that Zeena plans to travel to Bettsbridge to see a new doctor, and she will have to stay there overnight. He is excited at the prospect of spending a night alone with Mattie. So as not to lose any time together with Mattie, Ethan tells Zeena that he will not be able to drive her to the station because he needs to ask the owner of the general store for a cash advance on his lumber.

During this time Ethan thinks about how he came to marry Zeena in the first place. He first met Zeena, a distant cousin on his mother's side, when she came to the Frome household to nurse his ailing mother. Depressed by his mother's subsequent death and the thought of spending a winter alone on the farm, Ethan is reminded of the extent to which Zeena brought life and a small degree of happiness into a house full of sickness and death. He proposed marriage at a time when he was weak and grieving, and Zeena promptly changed from a strong, happy woman into a sickly, complaining shrew. Since his marriage, Ethan has been trapped in Starkfield because Zeena had no desire to take on the challenge of moving to a city, where there might have been more opportunities for her husband. Zeena is the kind of person who fears being lost in the sheer size of a city. So she chooses to remain in Starkfield because she can "look down on Starkfield," while on the other hand "she could not have lived in a place which looked down on her."

Having had his plea for a cash advance turned down by Andrew Hale, the owner of the general store, he returns home to have dinner with Mattie. They pass a pleasant evening together, but during the dinner Zeena's cat knocks over and breaks a red pickle dish that Zeena usually keeps stored away in a cupboard. The dish was a wedding present, and thus has a special meaning for Zeena. Both Ethan and Mattie know she will be furious when she finds out it is broken. It somewhat dampens the mood of the dinner, but Ethan hits on the plan of buying some glue and mending it the next day, before Zeena returns. After Mattie cleans up the kitchen and sits in Zeena's rocking chair, Ethan reflects on how content he is and begins to imagine a life together with Mattie.

The next day Zeena returns before he can buy glue in town and mend the dish. Zeena then reveals to Ethan the doctor's diagnosis that she is "sicker" than even she had thought. Consequently, Zeena has hired a "girl" to enable her to avoid even the minimal amount of housekeeping she had formerly done. In response to Ethan's angry, sarcastic questions as to how they are going to pay for a servant since they barely survive as it is, Zeena replies that Ethan can pay her with the money he was supposedly paid in advance for the lumber. Having neatly caught him out when he admits to not having the money, Zeena then drops her bombshell: With the hiring of the servant girl, Mattie's services will no longer be required, and she will have to leave almost immediately. Ethan, completely outmaneuvered and overpowered by Zeena, cannot shake her resolve. Later that evening Zeena discovers the broken dish, and Mattie confesses that she used it. This episode seems to seal Mattie's fate, and Ethan, in his helplessness and powerlessness, sees how desolate and lonely his life will be without her.

That night Ethan considers his options. For a while he entertains the notion of leaving Zeena the farm, escaping to the West with Mattie, and starting over. However, he soon realizes that he barely has the money for the train fare, and the proceeds from the sale of the farm would not be enough to support Zeena. In a crushing moment, he sees the depressing facts of his life: He is, and always has been, completely trapped in a web of commitments and obligations to others, and escape is impossible. Morning comes and Ethan hits on a last ditch effort to raise enough money to abandon Zeena for Mattie. He considers asking Andrew Hale, who had earlier refused him an advance on his lumber, for the advance again, this time under the pretext of his wife's illness and her taking on a hired girl. With this money, Ethan reasons, he and Mattie can make good their escape West and leave Zeena's family to take care of his wife. However, on the road he meets Hale's wife, who kindly sympathizes with how hard his life has been since his father first became ill and set in motion the events that left him trapped in Starkfield. Feeling that he would be deceiving the kindly and sympathetic Hales, and seeing for the first time how cruel it would be to abandon Zeena, he finally accepts that Mattie will be leaving without him.

Later that morning Ethan insists on taking Mattie to the train station. He takes a longer route, stopping at a place where, the previous summer, he and Mattie had attended a church picnic together. It was there that they had felt the first stirrings of their unspoken love for each other. Before the train comes, Ethan insists on taking Mattie for a sled ride down School House Hill, something he had promised her the night of the dance. After the first ride down, they kiss, and all of their repressed feelings for each other suddenly come out in a flood of words. Ironically, though, the moment that their love for each other is finally brought out into the open is the very moment that Mattie is forced to leave. They both realize that they cannot possibly bear to live apart; yet there is no way they can live together. In a climactic moment, Mattie proposes a suicide pact. They will take another sled run down the hill and steer the sled into the elm tree at the bottom. Ethan eventually agrees, but just before the sled hits the tree, "his wife's face, with twisted monstrous lineaments, thrust itself between him and his goal." It is as if Zeena is, by sheer force of will, working to thwart their plan. To communicate Zeena's evil power over Ethan and Mattie, the plan fails: Both are seriously crippled but survive.

The story now returns to the "present" as the narrator walks into the Frome's living room. In a tragic twist to the plot, we see that the crippled Mattie has in effect replaced Zeena and has become the complaining, querulous burden that Ethan's wife once was. Zeena, it transpires, mysteriously regains her health upon hearing of the accident and spends her days nursing Mattie, as she once nursed Ethan's mother. Ethan, of course, has remained caught between these two women while their respective roles have reversed themselves; however, he is still charged with the burden of having to eke out a living from his ramshackle farm to provide for them both. The essential difference now, though, is that he no longer has any hopes, and he is crippled in body as well as in spirit.

THE CHARACTERS

Ethan Frome. The protagonist, whose personal circumstances constitute the central drama of the novel. Due to the fact that he has a sensitive, generous-spirited nature that is subjugated by his mean-spirited, petty wife, Zeena, Ethan is in many ways the typical kind of antihero common to Wharton's fiction. Once Ethan had a passion for science and enough ambition to begin studying at a technical college. As a young adult, we find out that "he had always been more sensitive than the people about him to the appeal of natural beauty. His unfinished studies had given form to this sensibility and even in his unhappiest moments field and sky spoke to him with a deep and powerful persuasion." The potential for growth that is embedded in his character and nature is contrasted with the hard facts of his present circumstances: at fifty-two years of age, he is half crippled and barely earns a living on his small farm and sawmill. Thus, the contrast between what Ethan is and what he could have been is the true tragedy of this novel. This tragedy is compounded by the narrator's reconstructed tale of his thwarted love for Mattie Silver, with whom Ethan might have fulfilled his potential for spiritual and intellectual growth. As it is, Ethan has become a grim, isolated figure whose outer appearance as a crippled "ruin of a man" communicates the outcome of all he had hoped to achieve in life.

Mattie Silver. A cousin of Ethan's wife, Zeena. Due to her father's bankruptcy, subsequent death, and the revelation of his scandalous financial conduct, Mattie was left homeless. She was taken in by the Frome's as a housekeeper and nurse to Zeena. Mattie, like Ethan, has a generous and sensitive nature, which in turn has a positive effect on Ethan: "She had an eye to see and an ear to hear: he could show her things and tell her things, and taste the bliss of feeling that all he imparted left long reverberations and echoes he could wake at will." What Mattie as a character conveys more than anything is a sense of vitality and an energetic optimism. These qualities stand in stark contrast to Zeena Frome and allow the reader to see what Ethan might have become if he had married someone such as Mattie, who possesses many of his own best qualities. Like Ethan, she too is crippled by the suicide attempt on the sled run, showing again what has become of a character who had the potential to live a much more fulfilled life.

Zeena Frome. Ethan's wife. Zeena once nursed Ethan's mother on her deathbed, and she married Ethan after his mother died. Soon after their marriage, Zeena became sickly, manipulative, and demanding, yet we never know how she became sick or what it is she suffers from. Wharton makes Zeena as petty, scheming, and fundamentally evil as possible, and she wants us to feel she is responsible for Ethan's entrapment in Starkfield. Somehow she has made Ethan old before his time, and we are told that, "though she was but seven years her husband's senior, and he was only twenty-eight, she was already an old woman." Zeena is a fascinating character because, in spite of her sickliness, she manages to wield complete power over Ethan. Perceiving what a threat Mattie is to her marriage, Zeena successfully schemes to get rid of her. After the sledding accident, Zeena's power over Mattie is total, and she dominates Ethan more than ever. Strangely, she also regains her health in the wake of Mattie's being crippled. Thus, it would appear that Zeena is the "winner" in this tragic tale, and she is certainly typical of a kind of character we see often in Wharton's fiction: one who, through small-minded scheming, manages to crush the will of a morally superior character.

Narrator. Ironically, the narrator is an engineer, which is what Ethan once wanted to become. While he is working temporarily in Starkfield, he is struck by the tragic demeanor of Ethan Frome and reconstructs the story of how Ethan came to be in such a predicament. His attitude toward Ethan is overwhelmingly sympathetic, marking him as one of Wharton's "sensitive" characters who can see the tragedy of those who are not allowed to fulfill their potential.

Harmon Gow. A resident of Starkfield who relates certain parts of Ethan's story to the narrator. For the narrator, though, Gow can only go "as far as his mental and moral reach permitted" in telling Ethan's story, which is why the narrator has to fill in the gaps.

Mrs. Ned Hale (formerly Ruth Varnum). The narrator lodges at Mrs. Ned Hale's home. A friend of Mattie Silver, Mrs. Hale adds some more details to the narrator's understanding of Ethan Frome's life.

Andrew Hale. The owner of a Starkfield construction company, he refuses Ethan a fifty-dollar advance on the lumber Ethan brings him from the Frome mill. Ethan thinks of Andrew Hale as a kindly man and considers asking him for the advance later in the novel so that he can escape with Mattie.

Ned Hale. The eldest son of Andrew Hale. He is courting Ruth Varnum at the time of the sledding "accident."

Mrs. Andrew Hale. Her conversation with Ethan on the morning of Mattie's intended departure from Starkfield shows her sympathy for Ethan's predicament. However, her kindliness convinces Ethan that he could not possibly deceive her husband by using the lumber advance to run away with Mattie.

Dennis Eady. The young son of a well-to-do grocer in Starkfield, he appears at the town dance with Mattie Silver. He tries to court her, but she turns down his advances.

Jotham Powell. A hired laborer on the Frome farm.

CHAPTER 1

The Sources and Setting of *Ethan Frome*

READINGS ON
ETHAN FROME

Autobiographical Sources

R.W.B. Lewis

R.W.B. Lewis sees *Ethan Frome* as the creative culmination of three turbulent years in Wharton's personal life when her marriage to Teddy Wharton broke down and she both began and ended an affair with Morton Fullerton, an American journalist living in Paris. In Zeena Frome's sickness and Ethan's hopeless sense of entrapment, we see a fictional expression of the emotional and physical breakdown of Teddy Wharton and Edith Wharton's fear that she would never escape her suffocating marriage. Besides his definitive biography of Edith Wharton, R.W.B. Lewis is also the author of the classic study of nineteenth-century American literature, *The American Adam: Innocence, Tragedy, and Tradition in the Nineteenth Century* (1955).

Sending [art critic and close friend Bernard] Berenson greetings at Christmas, Edith remarked that the new year of 1911 "owes us all something, don't you think?" In fact, by this time she was in surprisingly good spirits. Her health had much improved; she had recovered her "lost balance"; and she was working again after many "wasted months"—working steadily, and working better than she had for a long time. She had begun a "new opus," and it was proving enormously stimulating.

Tales of Men and Ghosts had come out in October to a mixed and even a confused reception. It contained one small masterpiece, "The Eyes," and another ghost story, "Afterward," which begins promisingly but wilts into melodrama; and several other tales not without interest, such as "The Letters," "His Father's Son," and "The Debt." Some reviewers dismissed them all as no better than run-of-the-mill magazine fiction; others, on the contrary, accused Wharton

Excerpted from *Edith Wharton: A Biography*, by R.W.B. Lewis. Copyright © 1975 by Harper and Row, Publishers, Inc. Reprinted by permission of HarperCollins Publishers, Inc.

of an excess of subtlety beyond anything the average magazine reader could enjoy. The latter charge, it might be said, could be justifiably leveled against "The Blonde Beast," whose Nietzschean title [in the style of philosopher and poet Friedrich Nietzsche] is only skimpily fulfilled in the story, which has to do (apparently) with an unprincipled young man acquiring a moral sense. Edith agreed . . . that she had failed to pull it off—that "it *was* a good subject," but she had written it at a bad moment. The volume sold about four thousand copies, the figure around which her collections tended to hover.

THE ORIGINS OF *ETHAN FROME*

The new opus was called *Ethan Frome*, and it had its origins in an exercise she had written—probably in 1907—for her French teacher in Paris. In *A Backward Glance*, Edith Wharton recalled that when she first settled in Paris, she became aware that her spoken French derived largely from her reading in seventeenth-century literature, so much so that [French poet, novelist, and critic Paul-Charles-Joseph] Bourget teased her for speaking "the purest Louis Quatorze." She asked [French critic] Charles du Bos to find some young professor who could help her bring her idiom up to date. The amiable youth who took on the job suggested she prepare an "exercise" before each visit. For Edith, this meant writing a story, and for a few weeks she plodded ahead with what would be the French seed of *Ethan Frome*. The lessons were given up and the copybook mislaid; but the basic motif returned to her mind in December 1910.

The exercise, untitled, dealt with an impoverished New England farmer named Hart, married to an ailing and complaining wife, and in love with his wife's niece Mattie. Anna, the wife, of a sudden, declares that Mattie must be sent away. Hart offers to go with her, but Mattie, insisting in tears that Anna had been kinder to her than any other relation, refuses to let him do so. Out of this fragile piece of fiction Edith Wharton kept the basic situation and a part of its development, one proper name, and a few telling images and details.

When Edith began writing *Ethan Frome*, she conceived of it as a longish short story to be finished in no more than a fortnight; she was amused and surprised at the way it grew under her hands. Soon after the first of the year, she told Berenson:

I am driving harder and harder at that ridiculous nouvelle, which has grown into a large long-legged hobbledehoy of a young novel. 20,000 long it is already, and growing. I have to let its frocks down every day, and soon it will be in trousers! However, I see the end.

She had gotten past "the hard explanatory part" (the sketching in of the backgrounds of the three central characters), "and the *vitesse acquise* is beginning to rush me along." The scene, she said, "is laid at Starkfield, Mass., and the nearest cosmoplis is called Shadd's Falls. It amuses me to do that décor in the rue de Varenne."

When Berenson inquired about further progress on her "novel," Edith replied in late March: "My 'novel' doesn't deserve the name. It is a hybrid, or rather a dwarf form, of the species: scarcely 40,000 words." But when she received the proofs of her "winter's work" in April—the story was due to begin in the August *Scribner's*—she confessed to being in a "state of fatuous satisfaction.". . .

INNER TURMOIL AND EXTERNAL EVENTS

Ethan Frome, which ran in *Scribner's* from August through October and was published in book form at the end of September, was in good part the product of Edith Wharton's personal life during the previous few agitated years. Into no earlier work of fiction, not even *The House of Mirth*, had she poured such deep and intense private emotions. *Ethan Frome* in this regard was a major turning point, whether or not it was also the very finest of her literary achievements. Edith had hitherto reserved her strongest feelings for poetry; henceforth, they would go into her novels and stories. The experience of writing the fictively conceived 1908 journal had served her well. From this moment forward, and with obvious exceptions, Edith Wharton's fictional writings began to comprise the truest account of her inward life.

One event external to her life also contributed to the climax of *Ethan Frome*. In March 1904 there had been a disastrous sledding accident at the foot of Courthouse Hill in Lenox (Schoolhouse Hill in the novella). Four girls and a boy, all about eighteen and all but one juniors in Lenox High School, had gone coasting after school on a Friday afternoon. They made several exuberant runs down the mile-long slope, a descent on which a tremendous momentum can be achieved. On their last flight the young people's "double-ripper" sled crashed into the lamppost at the bottom of the hill. One of the girls, Hazel Crosby, suffered multiple fractures and internal injuries; she died that evening. Lucy Brown had her thigh fractured and her head gashed, and was permanently lamed. Kate Spencer's face was badly scarred.

Ethan Frome, when the narrator meets him at the opening of the tale, walks painfully with a lameness that checked "each step like the jerk of a chain"; there is an angry red gash across his forehead. The story that Ethan eventually unfolds for his visitor, and that the latter pieces together from other sources, goes back nearly thirty years to events leading up to a sledding catastrophe.

As a young farmer in the New England village of Starkfield, Ethan had married an older woman, Zenobia, a morose figure victimized by real and imaginary ailments. Her cousin Mattie Silver had come to help with the household chores and the work on the hard-pressed farm. Ethan and Mattie, much of an age, fall in love, even while realizing that there is no future for the two of them together. When "Zeena" announces that Mattie is to be sent away and replaced by a more efficient housemaid, the lovers determine to kill themselves by crashing their sled into the tree at the foot of the hill near the main road. The attempt is hideously unsuccessful. Ethan is merely lamed and Mattie crippled for life. They live on now in the joyless ménage dominated by the abruptly recovered Zenobia.

A CLASSIC OF AMERICAN REALISM

In her description of the bleak village of Starkfield and the allusions to nearby places like Bettsbridge, Corbury Flats, and Corbury Junction, Edith Wharton was drawing upon her memory of Plainfield and Lenox, of the Berkshire scenes she had so frequently passed through on the drives to Ashfield and back. She was re-creating the spell that the New England landscape had laid upon her, its dark somber beauty, its atmosphere (for her) of the haunted and tragic.

The treatment both of setting and character shows Edith Wharton in perfect command of the methods of literary realism; in its grim and unrelenting way, *Ethan Frome* is a classic of the realistic genre. At the same time, it is Edith Wharton's most effectively American work; her felt affinities with the American literary tradition were never more evident. A certain Melvillian grandeur [the style of Herman

Melville] went into the configuration of her tragically conceived hero. Despite her early disclaimers, the spirit of Nathaniel Hawthorne pervades the New England landscape of the novella and lies behind the moral desolation of Ethan Frome—a desolation as complete in its special manner as that of his namesake, Hawthorne's Ethan Brand. The sense of deepening physical chill (the French translation was called *Hiver*) that corresponds to the inner wintriness is similarly Hawthornian in nature. The role of the inquisitive city-born narrator is deployed with a good deal of the cunning and artistry of [novelist] Henry James.

But the great and durable vitality of the tale comes at last from the personal feelings Edith Wharton invested in it, the feelings by which she lived her narrative. *Ethan Frome* portrays her personal situation, as she had come to appraise it, carried to a far extreme, transplanted to a remote rural scene, and rendered utterly hopeless by circumstance. As she often did, Edith shifted the sexes in devising her three central characters. Like Edith Wharton, Ethan Frome is married to an ailing spouse a number of years older than he, and has been married for about the same length of time as Edith had been tied to Teddy. Ethan sometimes wonders about Zeena's sanity, and he daydreams about her death, possibly by violence. . . . He looks about frantically for some avenue to freedom, but his fate is conveyed to him in Edith's regular image for her own condition: "The inexorable facts closed in on him like prison-warders handcuffing a convict. . . . He was a prisoner for life."

THE FULLERTON CONNECTION

The relationship between Ethan and Mattie Silver contains memories of Morton Fullerton (even the names echo faintly) and passages transposed from the 1908 journal. Ethan and Mattie go star charting together; he feels that for the first time in his life he has met someone who can share his sensitiveness to natural beauty. During their one evening together, he with his pipe and Mattie with her sewing, Ethan lets himself imagine—as Edith had done on a winter evening in the Rue de Varenne—that their evenings would always be so. But in the savage quarreling between Ethan and Zeena, in the latter pages of the story, we hear something of the bitter recriminations Edith and Teddy had begun to visit upon each other. And in the denouement—

where the bountifully healthy and vindictive Zeena commands a household that includes Mattie as a whining invalid and Ethan as the giant wreck of a man—we have Edith Wharton's appalling vision of what her situation might finally have come to.

THE RESPONSE TO *ETHAN FROME*

It was quickly recognized by reviewers that *Ethan Frome* was one of Edith Wharton's finest achievements, though some of them found the concluding image too terrible to be borne. The entire tale, said a writer in *The New York Times*, was an exercise in subtle torture. A library guide declared the book too pessimistic to be recommended to the general reader, and the critic in *The Bookman*—confusing Edith Wharton's judgment on life with her personal attitudes—could not forgive her her cruelty toward both her characters and her readers. But there was a great deal of praise, and almost every reviewer had admiring words for the story's construction and style.

Gratifying letters poured in on Edith. Dr. Kinnicutt told her prophetically that *Ethan Frome* was "a classic that will be read and re-read with pleasure and instruction," and was astonished at what she had been able to do in the midst of her "pressing anxieties." [Henry] James expressed total admiration. He had been jovially skeptical about the narrator's opening remark: "I had been sent by my employers . . ." the notion of dear Edith being sent anywhere by anyone, he commented, boggled belief. But when he finished the story he found, with his usual critical exactness, that it contained "a beautiful art and tone and truth—a beautiful artful kept-downness." Others, if less eloquent, were equally warm in their enthusiasm.

The New England Setting

Barbara A. White

Edith Wharton set most of her novels and stories in
New York and Europe, but Barbara A. White notes that
some of her strongest writing used the New England
setting, and that New England itself was a significant
factor in Wharton's life. White sees a consistency in
Wharton's choice of New England's people and places
as the background for her fiction. While her portrayals
of fashionable New York and Europe dissect the social
rituals and hypocritical morals of an exclusive kind of
society, Wharton used New England to explore psychological questions and the grimmer aspects of life.
Barbara A. White is a professor of English at the University of New Hampshire, and has edited a collection
of Edith Wharton's New England stories.

In her autobiography, *A Backward Glance* (1934), Edith
Wharton tells us that her colonial ancestors lived first in
Massachusetts. But they soon "transferred their activities to
the easier-going New York, where people seem from the out-
set to have been more interested in making money and acquiring property than in Predestination and witch-burning."
By the time Edith was born in 1862 her family fortunes had
long been amassed, and she would grow up to become a
leading chronicler of monied and propertied New York. Indeed, after she died in 1937, many critics would consider
"old New York" her proper subject and the novels that describe it, *The House of Mirth* (1905) and the Pulitzer
Prize–winning *The Age of Innocence* (1920), her most en-
during fictions.

But a part of Edith Wharton was always fascinated by the
land of predestination and witch-burning that her ancestors
fled. She set a surprising amount of her work in New England,

Excerpted from Barbara A. White, ed., Introduction to *Wharton's New England: Seven
Stories and* Ethan Frome. Copyright © 1995 by the Trustees of the University of New
Hampshire. Reprinted by permission of the publisher, the University Press of New En-
gland, Hanover, N.H.

from the stories that began her writing career to the novella
that gained lasting fame, *Ethan Frome* (1911), a wintery tale
of "Starkfield," Massachusetts. Recently the excellent but
long neglected *Summer* (1917) has been recognized as a
worthy companion piece to *Ethan Frome,* Wharton's "hot
Ethan," as she called it. Both *Ethan Frome* and *Summer* are
set in the Berkshires near Lenox, Massachusetts, where
Edith and her husband Teddy built an elegant house, the
Mount. Chafing from the restrictions of her life as a society
matron in New York, Edith considered the Mount "my first
real home"; she describes it lyrically in *A Backward Glance,*
recalling visits by Henry James and other friends.

THE IMPORTANCE OF NEW ENGLAND IN EDITH WHARTON'S WORK

Wharton used the western Massachusetts setting not only
for *Ethan Frome* and *Summer* but also for a novel, *The Fruit
of the Tree* (1907), and in numerous short stories throughout
her career. Long after the Mount was sold, the Whartons divorced, and Edith living out her life in Paris, Starkfield
would appear in "Bewitched" (1925). The last story Wharton
sent to her publishers before her death was "All Souls'"
(1937), another New England witch tale, and she left a number
of unpublished fragments with New England settings. A full
quarter of Wharton's eighty-five published short stories are
set in New England. Of these, three stories, "The Angel at the
Grave" (1901), "Xingu" (1911), and "All Souls'", are rated
among her very best.

That Wharton felt considerably attached to her New England body of work is shown by the fierceness with which
she defended it from attack. Although most reviewers
praised her treatment of New England, some thought her
settings too bleak—as in *Ethan Frome* and the short story
"The Pretext" (1908); others found mistakes, as in her de-
piction of factories in *The Fruit of the Tree.* Wharton seldom
responded to negative reviews, but she was stung by criti-
cisms that she was an outsider who knew nothing of New
England. . . .

EDITH WHARTON'S NEW ENGLAND BACKGROUND

Wharton was certainly correct about her familiarity with
New England. She had summered in the region since childhood in her parents' Newport, Rhode Island, mansion, and

as an adolescent she made visits to Bar Harbor, Maine, where she met her lifelong friend Walter Berry. The man she chose to marry was a Bostonian and Harvard graduate; in fact, all the men closest to her—her husband Teddy, Berry, her lover Morton Fullerton, and her art critic friend Bernard Berenson—were Harvard grads, however cosmopolitan and European-oriented they seemed. After her marriage Wharton bought and refurbished a house in Newport, which she named Land's End as it looked out to sea. She became acquainted with Boston through visits to her in-laws, and Teddy's mother also had a summer house in Lenox, Massachusetts. It was thus that Edith found a way to escape the humid climate and (in her view) anti-intellectualism of Newport.

In the eyes of some, Lenox was simply Newport in the mountains. It had become a fashionable resort for the nouveau riche, who lived in million dollar "cottages" and built castles with a hundred rooms. With some of these socialites Wharton would not be very popular. Her friend D.B. Updike, founder of the Merrymount Press in Boston, recalled that her neighbors "were sometimes made uncomfortable by the suspicion—by no means unfounded—that Mrs. Wharton was ironically amusing at their expense. I remember one evening in particular when she returned from a dinner remarking, 'The XYZ's have decided, they tell me, to have books in the library.'" Once when a dowager was showing off her house and gushed, "I call this my Louis Quinze room," Wharton reportedly replied, "*Why*, my dear?"

But in spite of the XYZ types, Wharton found fewer of Newport's social "inanities," as she put it, in Lenox, and she was intrigued by its literary past. Both Hawthorne and Melville had tramped through the Berkshires and described the area in their works, and one of America's pioneer novelists, Catharine Maria Sedgwick (1789–1867), hailed from nearby Stockbridge. Although Wharton tended to distance herself from her female forerunners, as shown in her remarks on [new novelists Sarah Orne Jewett and Mary] Wilkins Freeman, she used Sedgwick's life as a source for an unfinished novel, "The Keys of Heaven," which was set in a town called "Slowbridge."

LIFE AT LENOX

Wharton spent every summer from 1899 through 1908 in Lenox; in her words, "There for over ten years I lived and gardened and wrote contentedly." The Mount, the home she designed and built to her specifications, was completed in 1902. Although not as costly and ostentatious as the neighboring abodes, it still dwarfed Henry James's description—"a delicate French chateau mirrored in a Massachusetts pond" The Mount, which still stands today and can be visited, is an imposing four-story white stucco building with enough space to house a dozen servants. From the living and dining rooms of the ground floor, French doors lead to a terrace that once overlooked Wharton's profuse flower gardens. To many visitors the gardens were more impressive than the house. Wharton regularly won prizes for her flowers and once confided, "I'm a better landscape gardener than novelist, and this place, every line of which is my own work, far surpasses the *House of Mirth.*"

Wharton was not exactly a "summer visitor" and the Mount a summer home, for she usually spent half the year in Lenox, from June to December (and the other half in New York and Europe). She also participated in village activities, such as rearranging the Lenox Library and serving on the Village Improvement and the Flower Show committees. In ten years she spent a good deal of time in the area, and it was not her choice to leave it. But the Mount became a casualty of the Whartons' marital difficulties: Teddy refused to help manage the estate unless Edith retained him as her trustee; this she declined to do because he had embezzled some of her money to set up a mistress. Thus in 1911 the property was sold, and Edith removed permanently to Europe. Although she felt a "great ache" for the Mount, she was not to see Lenox again except as she re-created it in her fiction.

While living at the Mount, Wharton's pattern was to write in the mornings and spend the afternoons gardening, walking, doing village committee work, or hosting an endless stream of visitors. Most important for her writing was her habit of entertaining visitors with rides through the Berkshires, in the early years by horseback or carriage and later, when the Whartons had acquired an American car, by automobile. Henry James spoke fondly of these auto rides, and Wharton's biographer notes that "as they drove slowly through the little New England villages, Edith regaled the fascinated James with reports that had reached her about the dark unsuspected life—the sexual violence, even the incest—that went on behind the bleak walls of the farmhouses." James was not the only friend with whom Wharton

shared her interest in her less wealthy, year-round neighbors. D.B. Updike recalled one windy afternoon when they
drove past "a battered two-story house, unpainted, with a neglected dooryard tenanted by hens and chickens, and a few
bedraggled children sitting on the stone steps. 'It is about a
place like that,' said Mrs. Wharton, 'that I mean to write a
story. Only last week I went to the village meeting-house in
Lenox and sat there for an hour alone, trying to think what
such lives would be, and some day I shall write a story about
it.'"

   Eventually she would write more than one story. These
leisurely rides through the New England countryside (the
speed limit was twenty miles per hour and the car often
broke down) seem to have deeply inspired Wharton. While
her fiction based in Newport tends to be brittle social comedy, and except for the description of Newport in *The Age of
Innocence* inferior to her other work, her Lenox observations
stimulated her imagination and remained vivid in her mind.
Wharton toured with Updike in 1905, but she composed
Ethan Frome with "the greatest joy and the fullest ease" in
1911 and as late as 1916 wrote *Summer* "at a high pitch of
creative joy, but amid a thousand interruptions, and while
the rest of my being was steeped in the tragic realities of the
war; yet I do not remember ever visualizing with more intensity the inner scene, or the creatures peopling it."

THE WEALTHY "OUTSIDER"

From Wharton's perspective, her auto trips through the
Berkshires, and even as far away as Boston, New Hampshire,
and Maine, only proved her knowledge of New England.
One could, however, take another view of Edith Wharton
and guest being chauffeured through the countryside in her
luxurious car while they peered at the rustics, trying to envision the inside of a dilapidated farmhouse. This is the pose
of the outsider. It could easily be argued that even if Wharton resided in New England, her class status kept her from
truly knowing it: she was perhaps an aristocrat gone slum-
ming and her New England "a seasonal landscape through
which one drove with Henry James." Wharton was bound to
make mistakes, however much she researched local customs and events, and recent critics have found an increasing
number of "errors" in Wharton's work. It has been said of
Ethan Frome, for instance, that Ethan should deliver boards

instead of logs, shouldn't shave before he milks the cows, wouldn't waste time coasting downhill, and would never have allowed Mattie to attend a church dance, if there had been such things.

Of course, for every critic who complains that Wharton was an Episcopalian and failed to understand rural Christianity, there are several for whom the dance at the church glows in the imagination. It is important to ask whether Wharton had the desire or intent to portray New England in the thorough, balanced manner of the so-called "local colorist." Rather, she seems to have used New England settings for her own more Hawthornean purposes, as symbolic means of exploring favorite subjects, such as the absence of high culture in modern life, the permeation of the present by the past, and the claustrophobia of female experience. Wharton's New England fiction is most easily characterized by what it is *not* about, not like *The House of Mirth* and *The Age of Innocence* primarily about marriage and divorce, the dishonesty of the socioeconomic system, the power of society to mold individual lives, the turning of women into beautiful objects. With the exception of some Newport stories, it is less socially dense than her other work, more inclined to the probing of psyches than the dissection of manners. . . .

Finally, in the chilling *Ethan Frome* and her New England ghost stories ("The Triumph of Night," "Bewitched," and "All Souls'"), Wharton undertakes to scare us; she uses barren settings and cold and snow imagery to create haunting tales shadowed by isolation, crime, and incest. What holds this wide-ranging body of work together are the themes that Wharton sometimes wrote about in her other work but associated most strongly with New England: poverty and decay, moral intolerance ("witch-burning"), cultural emptiness, and oppression by the past.

A LOVE-HATE RELATIONSHIP WITH NEW ENGLAND

Poverty and decay are the hallmarks of Wharton's New England. She was clearly less interested in the mansions of her peers than the unpainted farmhouses with bedraggled children on the steps. In her early work the poverty often seems exaggerated, as in "Friends" (1900), one of her first stories set in New England. The heroine's friend lives in a shabby hovel in coastal Sailport while she struggles to support a "crippled" brother and "slatternly" sister. The town is described as a sort of wasteland—the streets are full of dust and garbage, and even "the patches of ground between the houses are not gardens, but waste spaces strewn with nameless refuse." Wharton's emphatic opening line, "Sailport is an ugly town," recalls her comment that she sought to avoid the rose-colored glasses of her forerunners. . . . At the beginning of her career, Wharton feared being pigeonholed as a "woman writer" or "local colorist," and along with such male authors as Theodore Dreiser and Stephen Crane, she wanted to announce her departure from the genteel, or rose-colored, tradition in American letters. Thus the exaggerated grimness of Sailport. An early version of the story was in fact rejected for being too negative, and Wharton had to promise her publisher to tone down "the *squalid* part."

Wharton's portrayal of a decaying New England was realistic to some extent, however. The region's population was shifting westward and into large cities, leaving behind empty farms; the once great seafaring centers, such as Portsmouth, New Hampshire, lost their power and riches. At the time Wharton began to publish, Boston had already been supplanted by New York as the literary center of the country. Young people made their way in the world by moving out of New England. Thus Wharton could accurately have an old-timer say of Ethan Frome: "Guess he's been in Starkfield too many winters. Most of the smart ones get away." Only Frome's obligation to care for his invalid parents, and later his wife, keeps him from abandoning his "stark field" for greener pastures. At the end of "Friends" the young heroine follows the path of Wharton's ancestors and moves to New York; there is no doubt that this is supposed to be a happy ending.

As her career progressed, Wharton was less insistent about describing New England as a rubbish heap, but the New England–New York contrast appears in many early tales. Generally the comparison is not very favorable to New England. Although in her life Wharton often felt she was escaping her native city for a relatively quiet and beautiful New England, she strikes a different balance in her fiction. It follows the same pattern as her autobiographical statement about her ancestors: New York is making money and having fun; New England is being poor and burning witches. . . .

ETHAN FROME AND NEW ENGLAND

Black on black could describe *Ethan Frome* and Wharton's New England ghost stories, where there is little comic relief. In *Ethan Frome* the protagonist is overcome by the same dark features Wharton attributes to New England in her earlier short stories: grinding poverty, cultural emptiness, and the oppression of a Puritan past. Ethan Frome's poverty, in the form of his "barren farm and failing saw-mill," keeps him from realizing his dream of leaving Starkfield for a larger place. Even before he falls in love with Mattie Silver and yearns for the money to take her away, "he had always wanted to be an engineer, and to live in towns, where there were lectures and big libraries." Starkfield lacks even the consolation of a visiting Osric Dane. Ethan's situation, Wharton indicates, is made particularly painful by the denial of his intellectual aspirations. Before his father's death he had studied engineering at a college in Worcester. Now he expresses "resentment" at his ignorance of scientific advances. Ethan has a great sensitivity to the quiet and beauty of his environment, but like Wharton herself he cannot tolerate the "mental starvation." As much as she loved the Mount, we recall, she could not stay there all year. "I am wretched at being in town," she would tell Sally Norton. "Oh, to live in the country all the year round." But then she would have missed the "mental refreshment" she found in New York and Europe.

Of course it is not only Ethan's poverty that traps him in Starkfield but also his moral scruples. He left college to care for his invalid mother and missed selling the farm and moving to a larger town because of Zeena's illness early in their marriage. As he contemplates going West with Mattie, he recalls that "he was a poor man, the husband of a sickly woman, whom his desertion would leave alone and destitute; and even if he had had the heart to desert her he could have done so only by deceiving two kindly people who had pitied him." The latter are Mr. and Mrs. Hale, from whom Ethan considers borrowing money but rejects the idea because he would be taking advantage of their sympathy in order "to obtain money from them on false pretenses." Here Ethan seems to be making it a moral issue whether the mutton should be roasted or boiled. Although Wharton clearly wants us to admire Ethan's basic honesty and sense of responsibility for others (his positive New England traits), his refusal to budge an inch in relation to the Hales makes him a "prisoner for life."

In Ethan's family graveyard stands a memorial to his ancestors, "ETHAN FROME AND ENDURANCE HIS WIFE, WHO DWELLED TOGETHER IN PEACE FOR FIFTY YEARS." The living Ethan wonders, in a bit of foreshadowing, whether the same epitaph will be written over him and Zeena. Everything repeats itself. It is no accident that Zeena originally came to the Fromes, as Ethan's cousin, to nurse his mother; then Mattie, Zeena's cousin, came to Nurse Zeena. Several times the women seem to Ethan to eerily change places, as when Mattie replaces Zeena on the threshold, repeating the previous evening, and Zeena's face "supersedes" Mattie's in the rocking chair. If the Starkfield women are interchangeable, we are prepared for the ghastly tableau at the end where the fresh and childlike Mattie has turned into Zeena. Mattie is now "witch-like," and critic Elizabeth Ammons has effectively interpreted *Ethan Frome* as a fairy tale in which poverty and isolation turn women into witches (and the men who stay, she might have added, into silent martyrs). The past bears down on the present and links Endurance Frome, with her Puritan name, to Ethan's mother, to Zeena, to Mattie. What seems so grim is not Ethan's or any one character's individual tragedy but the unbroken chain of want and despair.

THE IMPORTANCE OF THE WINTER LANDSCAPE IN *ETHAN FROME*

Fittingly, *Ethan Frome* takes place in winter (in its French version it was known as *L'hiver*). The ubiquitous snow makes the New England farmhouses even more isolated, and the chain of despair seems frozen into place. Wharton, who ranks with the greatest writers in her creation of setting and atmosphere, uses snow and cold to brilliant effect in creating a frightening, voidlike atmosphere. The narrator and Ethan are caught in one storm, for instance, in which the snow falls "straight and steadily from a sky without wind, in a soft universal diffusion. . . . It seemed to be a part of the thickening darkness, to be the winter night itself descending on us layer by layer." The colors of *Ethan Frome* are black and white, with the blank scary white of Herman Melville's Moby Dick and only a touch of color provided by Mattie's cheeks and the red pickle dish.

Wharton's snowy settings are organic and not just decorative. The snow becomes an agent in Ethan's unfolding story: it delays him in getting the glue for the broken pickle dish and leads inexorably to the sledding accident. Just as Ethan's maimed body is paralleled in his house, his emotions are mirrored in the frozen landscape. As the narrator describes him, "He seemed a part of the mute melancholy landscape, an incarnation of its frozen woe, with all that was warm and sentient in him fast bound below the surface." The snow is such a "smothering medium" that Ethan has buried his feelings, memories, and perhaps his will. He used to be able to remember his trip to Florida and in winter call up the sight of the sunlit landscape, "but now it's all snowed under." Ethan, "by nature grave and inarticulate," as Wharton tended to see New Englanders, finally lapses into silence in the same way that his mother stopped talking in her last years and Zeena eventually "fell silent." The silence seems to be that of the grave. No wonder Ethan "looks as if he was dead." The novella ends with Mrs. Hale's statement, "I don't see's there's much difference between the Fromes up at the farm and the Fromes down in the graveyard."

CHAPTER 2

Style, Technique, and Theme in *Ethan Frome*

READINGS ON
ETHAN FROME

Imagery and Symbolism Reinforce the Novel's Meaning

Kenneth Bernard

Kenneth Bernard writes that Wharton's use of imagery and symbolism in *Ethan Frome* allows her to indirectly communicate the intense conflicts and deeper sources of motivation in the novel's three main characters. What they invariably leave unsaid is richly complemented by the images associated with the setting, the use of light and dark in the novel, and the work's sexual symbolism. Kenneth Bernard taught at the University of Long Island and is the author of many essays on American literature and twentieth-century drama.

A common criticism of Edith Wharton's *Ethan Frome* is that it is too contrived. In the last analysis, the characters seem peculiarly unmotivated, put through their paces in a clever, but mechanical, way. Such an opinion can only be the result of a cursory reading.

It is true that the book has a kind of stylistic and organizational brilliance. But it is not merely a display; it is invariably at the service of plot and character. The nature of her subject imposed certain difficulties on Wharton, particularly her characters' lack of articulation. How could she, without over-narrating, get at a deep problem involving such characters when they do not speak enough to reveal that problem? Frome's character and his marital relationship are at the heart of the novel, but they are revealed only indirectly. Wharton solved her difficulty in a masterful way by her use of imagery and symbolism. It is in her use of imagery and symbolism that the depths of the story are to be found. Without an understanding of them, a reader *would* find the char-

Reprinted from Kenneth Bernard, "Imagery and Symbolism in *Ethan Frome*," *College English*, October 1961.

acters unmotivated and the tragedy contrived. For easy discussion, the imagery and symbolism may be divided into three parts: the compatibility of setting and character, the uses of light and dark, and the sexual symbolism. A survey of these three parts in the novel will, it is hoped, clarify the real story in *Ethan Frome* by adding a new dimension of meaning.

THE MEANING OF STARKFIELD

The beginning of this new dimension of meaning is the first mention of the New England village–Starkfield. On many levels the *locus* of the story is a stark field. The village lies under "a sky of iron," points of the dipper over it hang "like icicles," and Orion flashes "cold fires." The countryside is "gray and lonely." Each farmhouse is "mute and cold as a grave-stone." This characterization of Starkfield is consistent throughout the book. Frome, in all ways, fits into this setting. On several occasions his integration with it is described. The narrator, upon first seeing him, sees him as "bleak and unapproachable." Later he says of Frome, "He seemed a part of the mute melancholy landscape, an incarnation of its frozen woe, with all that was warm and sentient in him bound fast below the surface . . . he lived in a depth of moral isolation too remote for casual access." Frome, unhappily married to Zeena, and pining for her cousin Mattie, is indeed parallel to the Starkfield setting. Everything on the surface is hard and frozen. His feeling, his love, for Mattie cannot break loose, just as spring and summer are fast bound by winter's cold. Mattie, appropriately, has the effect of loosening the rigid physical and emotional landscape. At one point, when she speaks, "The iron heavens seemed to melt down sweetness." Again, she is "like the lighting of a fire on a cold hearth." Frome, however, who has suffered "the profound accumulated cold of many Starkfield winters," does not thaw easily. He remembers when his feelings were free, or, as he puts it, when he was once in Florida, climatically (and emotionally) the opposite of Starkfield: "Yes: I was down there once, and for a good while afterward I could call up the sight of it in winter. But now it's all snowed under." Finally there is Frome's inarticulateness. Not only are his feelings locked, frozen; his very speech is also, beyond the natural reticence of the local people. Neither he nor the landscape can express its warm and tender part. When

Mattie once pleases him immensely, he gropes "for a daz-
zling phrase," but is able to utter only a "growl of rapture:
'Come along.'" Later he is again thrilled by her: "Again he
struggled for the all expressive word, and again, his arm in
hers, found only a deep 'Come along.'" He is truly a man of
"dumb melancholy."

The separation of feeling from its expression, the idea of
emotion being locked away, separated, or frozen, just as
Starkfield is bound by ice and snow, is demonstrated also by
the Frome farm. The house seems to "shiver in the wind,"
has a "broken down gate," and has an "unusually forlorn
and stunted look." More important, though, is the "L." Wharton gives a full description of the New England farm "L":

> that long deep-roofed adjunct usually built at right angles to
> the main house, and connecting it, by way of store-rooms and
> tool-house, with the wood-shed and cow-barn. Whether be-
> cause of its symbolic sense, the image it presents of a life
> linked with the soil, and enclosing in itself the chief sources
> of warmth and nourishment, or whether merely because of
> the consolatory thought that it enables the dwellers in that
> harsh climate to get to their morning's work without facing
> the weather, it is certain that the "L" rather than the house it-
> self seems to be the center, the actual hearth-stone of the New
> England farm.

Frome casually mentions to the narrator that he had had to
take down the "L." Thus Frome's home is disjointed, separated from its vital functions, even as he is. The narrator, not
unnaturally, sees in Frome's words about the "diminished
dwelling the image of his own shrunken body." Just as
Frome is emotionally trapped, just as Starkfield is frozen in
the winter landscape, just as Frome's home is cut off from its
vitals, so too is he cut off physically from his former
strength, trapped in his crippled frame. Images of being
caught, bound, trapped are frequent. "He was a prisoner for
life." "It seemed to Ethan that his heart was bound with
cords which an unseen hand was tightening with every tick
of the clock." "I'm tied hand and foot, Matt." Although Mattie is described with flight images like "the flit of a bird in
branches," and birds making "short perpendicular flights,"
the last such image describing her is of her lashes beating
like "netted butterflies," and her last "twittering" is her pitiful cry after the unsuccessful suicide attempt, when she is a
broken, pain-racked body. Even Mattie, Frome's one hope of
escape, is trapped. On top of this, Frome mentions that be-

fore the railroad came to a nearby town the road by his farm was a main route, implying that business was better: "We're kinder side-tracked here now." The farm, too, is separated from its former economic vitality. Thus the setting of the novel, the landscape and the farm, is parallel to Frome's condition and serves to illuminate it. But Wharton does not stop at this point.

THE USE OF LIGHT AND DARK

There is hardly a page throughout the book that does not have some reference to light and dark. Wharton uses all of them with effect. The supreme light image is Mattie Silver, as her name implies. She is in contrast to everything in Starkfield; her feelings bubble near the surface. Frome, on the other hand, is all dark. He lives in the dark, especially emotionally. At the beginning of the novel, when he has come to meet Mattie, she is dancing gaily in a church filled with "broad bands of yellow light." Frome keeps "out of the range of the revealing rays from within." "Hugging the shadow," he stands in the "frosty darkness" and looks in. Later he catches up to her "in the black shade of the Varnum spruces," the spot from where they finally begin the attempted suicide that cripples them. He stands with her in "the gloom of the spruces," where it is "so dark . . . he could barely see the shape of her head," or walks with her "in silence through the blackness of the Hemlock-shaded lane." Blackness is his element. As they walk back to the farm he revels in their closeness. "It was during their night walks back to the farm that he felt most intensely the sweetness of this communion." Their love is a bloom of night. "He would have liked to stand there with her all night in the blackness." He does not see Mattie so much as sense her: ". . . he felt, in the darkness, that her face was lifted quickly to his." "They strained their eyes to each other through the icy darkness." Frome's favorite spot is a secluded place in the woods called Shadow Pond. On their last visit there "the darkness descended with them, dropping down like a black veil from the heavy hemlock boughs." Frome cannot seem to get out of the dark. And often, as in quotations above, the dark is pregnant with suggestions of death and cold. Frome's kitchen, on their return from the village, has "the deadly chill of a vault after the dry cold of night." As Ethan settles in his tomblike house, Mattie's effect on him dies away. He lies in bed and watches the light from her candle, which

> sending its small ray across the landing, drew a scarcely per-
> ceptible line of light under his door. He kept his eyes fixed on
> the light till it vanished. Then the room grew perfectly black,
> and not a sound was audible but Zeena's asthmatic breath-
> ing.

Without Mattie's "light" he is left with the ugly reality of his
wife. In numerous small ways also Wharton makes the light
and dark images work for her. When Mattie relieves Ethan's
jealousy at one point, "The blackness lifted and light flooded
Ethan's brain." When Mattie is told by Zeena she must go,
and she repeats the words to Ethan, "The words went on
sounding between them as though a torch of warning flew
from hand to hand through a dark landscape." Before their
suicide plunge, "The spruces watched them in blackness
and silence." A bitter argument between Ethan and Zeena is
"as senseless and savage as a physical fight between two enemies in the darkness." After, Zeena's face "stood grimly out
against the uncurtained pane, which had turned from grey
to black." The cumulative effect of all these images is to tell
us a great deal about Frome and his tortured psyche.

The most important thing the images of light and dark reveal about Frome is that he is a negative person. Frome is a
heroic figure: nothing less than the entire landscape can suf-
fice to describe him effectively; his agony is as broad and
deep as that of the winter scene. But he is not tragic because
he is a man of great potential subdued and trapped by forces
beyond his capacity. His tragedy is entirely of his own making. He is weak. His character never changes. Both before
and after the accident he is the same. Like his environment
he has a kind of dumb endurance for harsh conditions.
There are several indications of his weakness besides his
identity with darkness. Frome married Zeena because she
had nursed his mother through her final illness. He was
twenty-one and she twenty-eight. He married her less because he loved her than because he needed a replacement
for his mother. Certainly it is Zeena who cracks the whip in
the household, and Ethan who jumps. What Zeena says,
goes. Frome "had often thought since that it would not have
happened if his mother had died in spring instead of winter. . . ." When he and Mattie are about to attempt suicide,
Mattie sitting in front of Ethan on the sled, he asks her to
change places with him. She asks why. Quite sincerely he

answers, "Because I—because I want to feel you holding me." He wants to die being cuddled and comforted, leaving to Mattie the role of protector and shelterer.

Throughout the book, Frome recognizes his futility and accepts it rather than trying to fight his way out of it. He does not ever realistically reach for a solution. His love inspires little more than dreams. He thinks of another man who left his wife for another woman and invests the event with fairy tale qualities: "They had a little girl with fair curls, who wore a gold locket and was dressed like a princess." Once he imagines Zeena might be dead: "What if tramps had been there—what if. . . ." When he spends his one night alone with Mattie, instead of thinking of a way to achieve permanance for their relationship he "set his imagination adrift on the fiction that they had always spent their evenings thus and would always go on doing so. . . ." Ironically, this is just about what he achieves by crippling instead of killing himself and Mattie. He did not, however, envision that Zeena would be a necessary part of the arrangement, as a nurse to Mattie.

The negation, the blackness, in his character is revealed also in his funereal satisfactions. When Mattie says she is not thinking of leaving because she has no place to go, "The answer sent a pang through him but the tone suffused him with joy." He rejoices in her helplessness; he is pained and thrilled at the same time because she has nowhere to go, because she too is trapped. Looking at the gravestones on his farm that have mocked him for years ("We never got away— how should you?"), he rejoices: ". . . all desire for change had vanished, and the sight of the little enclosure gave him a warm sense of continuance and stability."

> "I guess we'll never let you go, Matt," he whispered, as though even the dead, lovers once, must conspire with him to keep her; and brushing by the graves, he thought: "We'll always go on living here together, and some day she'll lie there beside me."

The finest thought he can have is of the triangle going on forever, and then lying in the earth next to Mattie: "He was never so happy with her as when he abandoned himself to these dreams." Frome's aspirations do not finally go beyond darkness. His final acceptance of suicide is the culmination of his negative instincts: death is the blackest blackness.

SEXUAL SYMBOLISM

Although the meaningful use of light and dark is pervasive in the book and is illuminating, it is the sexual symbolism that cuts deepest. The sexual symbolism is more dramatic than the two elements already discussed because it revolves around the key scenes in the book, Ethan and Mattie's night together and Zeena's return. It is also more significant because without an understanding of it the source of Zeena and Ethan's estrangement and antagonism remains unknown. After all, what *is* the deep gulf that lies between them? There is no explicit revelation in the book. In part, Wharton's use of symbolism to clarify the book's central problem is compatible with the inarticulateness of the characters. But perhaps also it represents a reticence or modesty of the author's. Ethan and Mattie's night together is ostensibly a mild affair. Wharton might well have revealed then the true relationship between Frome and his wife and demonstrated overtly Mattie and Ethan's transgression. But was it really necessary for her to do so? Even as it is, the evening progresses with the greatest of intensity. Every action, every word, even every silence quivers. It is because these apparently innocent actions and words exist in such intensity that they must be scrutinized. There are disproportions of feeling, particularly centering around the pickle dish, that are revealing. A proper understanding of the events of that evening sheds light throughout the book, and particularly makes the light and dark imagery more meaningful.

Barrenness, infertility, is at the heart of Frome's frozen woe. Not only is his farm crippled, and finally his body too; his sexuality is crippled also. Zeena, already hypochondriac when he married her, has had the effect of burying his manhood as deeply as everything else in him. In seven years of marriage there have been no children. Within a year of their marriage, Zeena developed her "sickliness." Medicine, sickness, and death are, in fact, rarely out of sight in the book. The farm itself, with its separation of its vital center, its regenerative center, suggests of course the sexual repression. The name Starkfield also connotes barrenness. However, Ethan and Zeena's sexual relationship is suggested most by the incident of the pickle dish, a dish which, unless understood, lies rather unaccountably at the very center of the book.

The red pickle dish is Zeena's most prized possession. She

received it as a wedding gift. But she never uses it. Instead she keeps it on a shelf, hidden away. She takes it down only during spring cleaning, "and then I always lifted it with my own hands, so's 't shouldn't get broke." The dish has only ceremonial, not functional, use. The sexual connotations here are obvious. The fact that the wedding dish, which was meant to contain pickles, in fact never does, explains a lot of the heaviness of atmosphere, the chill, the frigidity. The most intense scenes of the book, the most revealing, center around this dish. For example, Zeena never does discover an affair in the making between Ethan and Mattie, nor does she ever say anything, except for one hint not followed up, that reveals such knowledge. Her only discovery (and it is *the* discovery of the book) is of her broken (and used) pickle dish. It is this which brings the only tears to her eyes in the entire book. When Zeena is gone for a day, Mattie, significantly, brings down and uses the pickle dish in serving Ethan supper. Only if the dish is properly understood can it be seen how her violation is a sacrilege, as Zeena's emotions amply testify. The dish is broken, and Ethan plans to glue it together. Of course the dish can never be the same. This kind of violation is irrevocable. Zeena does not discover that the dish is broken until she gets, again significantly, heartburn, the powders for which she keeps on the same private shelf as the pickle dish. The scene following is a symbolic recognition of the fact that Mattie has usurped her place, broken her marriage, and become one with Ethan, though in fact it was the cat (Zeena) who actually broke the dish. The fact that Zeena never truly filled her place, acted the role of wife, and is herself responsible for the failure of the marriage does not bother her. Ethan is hers, however ceremonially, and she resents what has happened. Her emotion transcends any literal meaning the dish may have, so much so that other implications of the dish force themselves on the reader. Speaking to Mattie, she says,

> ". . . you waited till my back was turned, and took the thing I set most store by of anything I've got, and wouldn't never use it, not even when the minister come to dinner, or Aunt Martha Pierce come over from Bettsbridge. . . . I tried to keep my things where you couldn't get at 'em—and now you've took from me the one I cared for most of all—" She broke off in a short spasm of sobs that passed and left her more than ever like the shape of a stone. . . . Gathering up the bits of broken glass she went out of the room as if she carried a dead body. . . .

The passage reveals most clearly the gulf between Ethan and Zeena. The body she carries out is the corpse of her marriage. The evening that Mattie and Ethan spend together, then, is not as innocent as it seems on the surface. That Mattie and Ethan's infidelity is so indirectly presented, whether because of Wharton's sense of propriety or her desire to maintain a minimum of direct statement, does not at all lessen the reality of that fact. If the overt act of infidelity is not present, the emotional and symbolic act is. The passage is full of passion; the moment, for example, when Frome kisses the edge of the piece of material Mattie is holding has climactic intensity.

The sterility of their marriage, Frome's emasculation, is represented elsewhere. For example, just before Zeena leaves for the overnight trip to a doctor, she finishes a bottle of medicine and pushes it to Mattie: "It ain't done me a speck of good, but I guess I might as well use it up. . . . If you can get the taste out it'll do for pickles." This is the only other mention of pickles in the book. Significantly, it is the last word in the chapter before the one devoted to Ethan and Mattie's night together. The action might be interpreted as follows: after Zeena has exhausted the possibilities of her medicine for her "trouble," she turns to sex—but she passes on that alternative to Mattie. Mattie may use the jar for pickles if she wishes. The action is a foreshadowing of Mattie's use of the pickle dish. In a sense, Zeena has urged her to that act, for she is abdicating the position of sexual initiative.

Again, in *Ethan Frome* each word counts. But there are some descriptions, obviously very particular, that do not fit in with any generalizations already presented. However, in the light of an understanding of the pickle dish incident, they are clarified. When Frome first points out his home, the narrator notes "the black wraith of a deciduous creeper" flapping on the porch. Deciduous means shedding leaves, or antlers, or horns, or teeth, at a particular season or stage of growth. Frome has indeed shed his manhood. Sexually he is in his winter season. Later, another vegetation is described on the porch: "A dead cucumber vine dangled from the porch like the crape streamer tied to the door for a death. . . ." A cucumber is no more than a pickle. The pickle dish is not used; the cucumber vine is dead. That it should be connected with crape (black) and death is perfectly logical in the light of what has already been discussed about

Frome. Frome's sexuality is dead. There is, of course, in all this the suggestion that Frome could revive if he could but reach spring, escape the winter of his soul. Mattie is his new season. At one point, where Mattie "shone" on him,

> his soul swelled with pride as he saw how his tone subdued her. She did not even ask what he had done. Except when he was steering a big log down the mountain to his mill he had never known such a thrilling sense of mastery.

Mattie, as Zeena never does, makes Ethan feel the springs of his masculinity. But he never overcomes the ice of accumulated Starkfield winters. His final solution is to merge himself with winter forever.

Thus Ethan Frome, when he plunges towards what he considers certain death, is a failure but not a mystery. His behavior is not unmotivated; the tragedy is not contrived. The very heart of the novel is Frome's weakness of character, his negation of life. Behind that is his true, unfulfilled, relationship with Zeena. Wharton's economy of language in the novel is superb. There is hardly a word unnecessary to the total effect. Her final economy is the very brevity of the book. It fits the scene and character. There were depths to plumb; her people were not simple. To overcome the deficiencies of their natural reticence (and perhaps her own), to retain the strength of the severe and rugged setting, particularly the "outcropping granite," she resorted to a brilliant pattern of interlocking imagery and symbolism, three facets of which have been outlined here, to create a memorable work. The reader of *Ethan Frome*, then, need not find it merely a technically successful work, a virtuoso performance. With an understanding of the imagery and symbolism he can look into the heart of the book and see characters as full-bodied people in the grip of overwhelming emotional entanglements. He is also in a position to see the book's true dimensions as tragedy.

The Narrator's Sensitivity Highlights the Novel's Themes

Joseph X. Brennan

Through a close reading of the text, Joseph X. Brennan argues that the heightened sensitivity and imagination of the narrator, who in effect creates the story,
is mirrored in the complex structure of the novel.
What emerges is an array of opposing images that
richly elaborate themes of conformity, freedom, and
entrapment, and lend greater shades of complexity to
the novel's characters. Joseph X. Brennan taught English at the University of Notre Dame and has published a number of articles on nineteenth- and
twentieth-century American fiction.

In her brief but illuminating introduction to *Ethan Frome*
Wharton directed the greater part of her attention to the
narrator-framework of the novel, which she presumably regarded as her chief problem and special achievement. Whatever her real convictions may have been concerning her solution, [literary critic] John Crowe Ransom is certainly right
in regarding the results as less than satisfactory. For the
close reader readily discerns that the engineer-narrator did
not really gather his story "bit by bit, from various people,"
but having been inspired by a few bare hints and scraps of
information, created his "vision" of what *might* have been
almost entirely out of the stuff of his vivid imagination. In
short, the narrator who presents himself as an engineer in
the realistic framework of the novel is actually a writer in
disguise with the technical skill of a professional novelist
and the sensibility of a poet; and his imaginative recon-
struction of Ethan Frome's story, in view of what little he
had to go by, is really no more than a brilliant fiction. Once

Excerpted from Joseph X. Brennan, "*Ethan Frome:* Structure and Metaphor," *Modern Fiction Studies*, vol. 7, no. 4 (Winter 1961–1962), pp. 347–56. Copyright © 1961 Purdue Research Foundation. Reprinted by permission of The Johns Hopkins University Press.

one recognizes this fact, however, that we have to deal here with an overt fiction within a fiction, "it is expedient, if not indeed necessary, to accept this arrangement as the very form of the novel and to analyze it as such. Hence the need for a close examination of the "vision" within the novel in relationship to its narrator as well as on its own terms.

THE NARRATOR AS POET

From the many descriptions of the setting which one encounters in both the narrative framework and the "vision" of the novel, it is clear that the engineer-narrator is not only intensely responsive to the beauty of the natural scene and the seasons, but has a distinct predilection also for rendering his response in imagistic or poetic language. In the framework, for example, we encounter such "picture-making" passages as the following:

> When the storms of February had pitched their white tents about the devoted village and the wild cavalry of March winds had charged down to their support: I began to understand why Starkfield emerged from its six months' siege like a starved garrison capitulating without quarter.

> About a mile farther, on a road I had never travelled, we came to an orchard of starved appletrees writhing over a hillside among outcroppings of slate that nuzzled up through the snow like animals pushing out their noses to breathe. Beyond the orchard lay a field or two, their boundaries lost under the drifts; and above the fields, huddled against the white immensities of land and sky, one of those lonely New England farm-houses that make the landscape lonelier.

Even in his imaginative account of Ethan's history, the narrator frequently sets the scene with the same flair for metaphor:

> Here and there a star pricked through, showing behind it a deep well of blue. In an hour or two the moon would push up over the ridge behind the farm, burn a gold-edged rent in the clouds, and then be swallowed by them. A mournful peace hung on the fields, as though they felt the relaxing grasp of the cold and stretched themselves in their long winter sleep.

> Under the open sky the light was still clear, with a reflection of cold red on the eastern hills. The clumps of trees in the snow seemed to draw together in ruffled lumps, like birds with their heads under their wings; and the sky, as it paled, rose higher, leaving the earth more alone.

The narrator's acute sensitivity to the beauty of nature, in fact, accounts for much that is profoundly moving and memorable in *Ethan Frome*, so thoroughly does it permeate the whole novel, framework and vision alike.

It is not surprising, therefore, that in projecting the character of Ethan the narrator has liberally endowed him with much the same sensitivity he himself possesses. Though there is not the slightest indication from any source of evidence to which the engineer has access that either Ethan or Mattie was especially sensitive to the beauties of nature, the narrator has so thoroughly imbued the two of them with this susceptibility that it both motivates and dominates their relationship; this becomes readily evident in the following key passage:

> He had always been more sensitive than the people about him to the appeal of natural beauty. His unfinished studies had given form to this sensibility and even in his unhappiest moments field and sky spoke to him with a deep powerful persuasion. But hitherto the emotion had remained in him as a silent ache, veiling with sadness the beauty that evoked it. He did not even know whether any one else in the world felt as he did, or whether he was the sole victim of this mournful privilege. Then he learned that one other spirit had trembled with the same touch of wonder: that at his side, living under his roof and eating his bread, was a creature to whom he could say: "That's Orion down yonder; the big fellow to the right is Aldebaran, and the bunch of little ones—like bees swarmin—they're the Pleiades. . . ." . . . And there were other sensations, less definable but more exquisite, which drew them together with a shock of silent joy: the cold red of sunset behind winter hills, the flight of cloudflocks over slopes of golden stubble, or the intensely blue shadows of hemlocks on sunlit snow. When she said to him once: "It looks just as if it was painted!" it seemed to Ethan that the art of definition could go no farther, and that words had at last been found to utter his secret soul.

This special sensitivity, shared equally by the narrator and his imagined characters, accounts, moreover, for the many skeins of imagery which pattern the envisioned story. It accounts, first of all, for the chief pattern of contrast which runs throughout this story, that between indoors and outdoors, between the house as the symbolic stronghold of moral convention and conformity, and the open countryside as symbolic of natural freedom and passional abandon. And it accounts also for the elaborate system of metaphorical characterization developed in direct relationship to this basic symbolic pattern.

Of the many natural objects and locations which constitute the pattern of outdoor imagery, the two black Norway spruces are surely the most important, since they provide the setting for the lovers' uttermost passion and final fatal resolve. In their symbolical dark shadows, indeed, the story of Ethan and Mattie's secret passion virtually begins and ends. When for the first time in Chapter II they stand together in this darkness, their deep mutual passion is no less intense, and all the more painful, for being unexpressed and forbidden:

> He slipped an arm through hers . . . and fancied it was faintly pressed against her side; but neither of them moved. It was so dark under the spruces that he could barely see the shape of her head beside his shoulder. He longed to stoop his cheek and rub it against her scarf. He would have liked to stand there with her all night in the blackness.

In Chapter IX, when they again stand together under these spruces, they give passionate avowal to that love, of which, but three nights earlier, there had been only mute intimations. And it is in this darkness, finally, a darkness now of utter hopelessness, that they resolve to die together. Thus the spruces both shelter their forbidden love and foreshadow its tragic ending, forming a kind of dark parentheses to the brief interlude of their passion.

In direct antithesis to the dark freedom which the out-of-doors provides is the atmosphere of moral restriction which pervades the lamplit kitchen. When Ethan mentioned to Mattie the next evening, as they sat together in the kitchen, that he had seen a friend of hers getting kissed under the Varnum spruces, Mattie "blushed to the roots of her hair" and replied "in a low voice, as though he had suddenly touched on something grave." The paragraph following upon this passage points up sharply the contrary psychological and symbolic implications of these contrasting locations.

> Ethan had imagined that his allusion might open the way to the accepted pleasantries, and these perhaps in turn to a harmless caress, if only a mere touch on her hand. But now he felt as if her blush had set a flaming guard about her. . . . He knew that most young men made nothing at all of giving a pretty girl a kiss, and he remembered that the night before, when he had put his arm about Mattie, she had not resisted. But that had been out-of-doors, under the open irresponsible night. Now, in the warm lamplit room, with all its ancient implications of conformity and order, she seemed infinitely farther away from him and more unapproachable.

Insofar as the narrator has imagined and set these scenes, this symbolic use of the Norway spruces directly reflects his informing sensibility. The characterization of Mattie and

Zeena, however, though ultimately derived from the narrator's sensibility also, nevertheless becomes the immediate responsibility of Ethan in the envisioned story, for it is through his sensibility and from his point of view that this vision is projected. The distinction, of course, is a logical rather than real one, since the two sensibilities are really only one.

MATTIE AND NATURE IMAGERY

The imagistic light in which both Mattie and Zeena are consistently regarded by Ethan, in any event, is directly related to this larger pattern of contrast. In Ethan's mind, it is interesting to note, Mattie is constantly associated with the most lovely and delicate objects in nature. Her face "always looked like a window that has caught the sunset"; "it was part of the sun's red and of the pure glitter of the snow"; and it "changed with each turn of their talk, like a wheat-field under a summer breeze." Noteworthy also are the descriptions of Mattie's hair. Seen from behind, as she carried a lamp before her, it looked to Ethan "like a drift of mist on the moon"; and while she washed the dishes, the steam tightened "her rough hair into little brown rings like the tendrils of the traveller's joy." To the touch of his lips, moreover, Ethan found that her hair was "soft yet springy, like certain mosses on warm slopes, and had the faint woody fragrance of fresh sawdust in the sun"; and later, "he looked at her hair and longed to touch it again, and to tell her that it smelt of the woods." In the most passionate scene under the spruces, finally, Ethan stroked her hair, wanting "to get the feeling of it into his hand, so that it would sleep there like a seed in winter."

Especially important, and even symbolic, is the frequent association of Mattie with birds: for Ethan, "the motions of her mind were as incalculable as the flit of a bird in the branches"; and "her hands went 'up and down above the strip of stuff, just as he had seen a pair of birds make short perpendicular flights over a nest they were building." To him, also, her voice was a "sweet treble," and "the call of a bird in a mountain ash was so like her laughter that his heart tightened and then grew large." Of particular interest, therefore, is the manner in which, after the smash-up, Mattie's whimpering is confused in Ethan's mind with the sound of both a bird and a field-mouse: "The stillness was so profound that he heard a little animal twittering somewhere nearby under the snow. It made a small frightened *cheep* like a field mouse. . . ." Since Zeena, as we shall see below, is consistently associated with and even identified by her cat, this shift from the image of the small bird, the eternal but more elusive quarry of cats, to that of the field mouse, their more defenseless prey, is obviously symbolic of Zeena's final victory over Mattie.

Reinforcing these principal associations of Mattie with nature are a number of related but subordinate images. During a summer picnic, for example, Mattie looked as "bright as a blackberry" to Ethan as she attended a "gipsy fire." Elsewhere in the novel, when she learned from Ethan that she was to be dismissed, she stood silent, "drooping before him like a broken branch"; and as they embraced shortly thereafter, he felt "her lashes beat his cheek like netted butterflies."

Into the characterization of Mattie, furthermore, the narrator has quite deliberately woven a streak of symbolic red; she is so frequently connected with this color, in fact, that by the end of the story her personality is vividly imbued with the passion, vibrancy, and daring nonconformity which red traditionally connotes. In the opening scene, for example, she is imagined wearing a "cherry-coloured 'fascinator,'" with "the colour of the cherry scarf in her fresh lips and cheeks"; and in anticipation of her night alone with Ethan, "through her hair she had run a streak of crimson ribbon." Later that evening "her cheeks burned redder" and she "blushed to the roots of her hair," setting "a flaming guard about her." Of particular import in this scene, moreover, is the "dish of gay red glass" which Mattie had taken down from the forbidden shelf of Zeena's special possessions. As an object of beauty and gaiety, which Zeena, significantly, had never used once since her wedding, this gay red dish suggests symbolically the pleasure and passion that Ethan had sought and Zeena had thwarted in their marriage. As Zeena's property by marriage and by right, it represents also, respecting Ethan and Mattie, a forbidden pleasure and illicit passion. The shattering of the red dish, moreover, clearly prefigures the final shattering of their limbs and ill-starred love.

IMAGISTIC CORRELATIVES FOR ZEENA

In direct contrast to this rendering of Mattie in terms of nature and vibrant reds, are the descriptions of Zeena suggesting the artificial, angular, and unhealthy. This contrast is

brought into sharpest focus in the following paralleled passages, in which, on successive evenings, first Zeena and
then Mattie let Ethan in at the back door:

> Against the dark background of the kitchen she stood up tall
> and angular, one hand drawing a quilted counterpane to her
> flat breast, while the other held a lamp. The light, on a level
> with her chin, drew out of the darkness her puckered throat
> and the projecting wrist of the hand that clutched the quilt,
> and deepened fantastically the hollows and prominences of
> her high-boned face under its ring of crimping-pins. . . .

> She drew aside without speaking, and Mattie and Ethan
> passed into the kitchen, which had the deadly chill of a vault
> after the dry cold of the night.

> She stood just as Zeena had stood, a lifted lamp in her hand,
> against the black background of the kitchen. She held the
> light at the same level, and it drew out with the same dis-
> tinctness her slim young throat and the brown wrist no big-
> ger than a child's. Then, striking upward, it threw a lustrous
> fleck on her lips, edged her eyes with velvet shade, and laid a
> milky whiteness above the black curve of her brows.

> She wore her usual dress of darkish stuff, and there was no
> bow at her neck; but through her hair she had run a streak of
> crimson ribbon. This tribute to the unusual transformed and
> glorified her. She seemed to Ethan taller, fuller, more wom-
> anly in shape and motion. She stood aside, smiling silently,
> while he entered, and then moved away from him with some-
> thing soft and flowing in her gait. . . . A bright fire glowed in
> the stove. . . .

In contrast to Mattie's vivid coloring and beauty, Zeena's
face was "drawn and bloodless," "grayish," and "sallow,"
with "fretful" "querulous lines"; her hair was "thin," her lips
"straight," her eyes "lashless," and her looks "queer." At table
she made a "familiar gesture of adjusting her false teeth before she began to eat," and she "always went to bed as soon
as she had her supper." Before going to bed, however, she
wrapped her head "in a piece of yellow flannel"; and then
she slept, breathing asthmatically, "her mouth slightly open,
her false teeth in a tumbler by the bed. . . ." In short, "she
was already an old woman."

Countering the metaphorical association of Mattie and
birds, moreover, is the more literal and obvious relationship
between Zenobia and her cat. In the long anticipated
evening of Zeena's absence, in fact, the cat directly becomes
her watchful surrogate: "The cat jumped into Zeena's chair
. . . and lay watching them with narrowed eyes." Subsequently

the cat creates the illusion of Zeena's presence rather eerily when it "jumped from Zeena's chair to dart at a mouse," setting the empty chair to a "spectral rocking." Earlier in the evening the cat had disrupted their happiness even more violently by breaking the red pickle-dish, the symbol of their forbidden passion. In its cunning, cruelty, and languid domesticity the cat indeed is the perfect representative of its mistress. It seems, too, that the stuffed owl in the parlor was introduced to further suggest Zeena's affinity for the artificial and predaceous. In any event nothing natural and beautiful seems to thrive in her domain of drugs and patent medicines; even the kitchen geraniums fade and "pine away." From the characterization of Zeena in both the narrative framework and the story proper, moreover, one is evidently intended to infer that she gathers a certain morbid strength from the weakness and illness of others: vulture-like she diligently attends the dying.

IMAGES THAT ENLARGE THE PRESENCE OF ETHAN

In close connection with this pattern of contrasts in the characterizations of Zeena and Mattie, there appears another set of contrasts in which Ethan himself figures. At the beginning of the novel, when the narrator first beholds Ethan, twenty-four years after his smash-up, the things which most impress him are his deep taciturnity and moral isolation, traits for which the frozen landscape most aptly suggests the verbal formulations:

> He seemed a part of the mute melancholy landscape, an incarnation of its frozen woe, with all that was warm and sentient in him fast bound below the surface. . . . I simply felt that he lived in a depth of moral isolation too remote for casual access, and I had the sense that his loneliness . . . had in it . . . the profound accumulated cold of many Starkfield winters.

It is interesting to note, therefore, that as the narrator envisions Ethan's relationship with Mattie, twenty-four years earlier, "she, the quicker, finer, more expressive, instead of crushing him by the contrast, had given him something of her own ease and freedom." And since she is most frequently associated with summer imagery, it is not surprising that as they make their way home the first evening, Ethan's growing conviction of their mutual love is paralleled by an imagistic progression from spring thaw to summer warmth and flow:

Her wonder and his laughter ran together like spring rills in a thaw.

The iron heavens seemed to melt and rain down sweetness.

They walked on as if they were floating on a summer stream.

The joyful anticipation of spending the evening alone with Mattie further unlocks Ethan from his wintry taciturnity: "he, who was usually so silent, whistled and sang aloud as he drove through the snowy fields. There was in him a slumbering spark of sociability which the long Starkfield winters had not yet extinguished." And sitting in the kitchen with Mattie that night, "he had a confused sense of being in another world, where all was warmth and harmony . . . ," so that, finally, "all constraint had vanished between the two, and they began to talk easily and simply." In their most passionate embrace two nights later under the Varnum spruces, this progression from wintry cold to summer heat reaches its culmination: "once he found her mouth again, and they seemed to be by the pond together in the burning August sun." The summer of their love, nevertheless, was destined from the first to be only a short one, to be almost the illusion of one: "all their intercourse had been made up of just such inarticulate flashes, when they seemed to come suddenly upon happiness as if they had surprised a butterfly in the winter woods."

In opposition to the imagistic warmth and ease characterizing his relationship with Mattie is the chill, numbness, and paralysis which typifies his relationship with his wife. Ironically it was Ethan's very dread of loneliness, silence, and isolation—all symbolically related to winter—that had induced him to marry Zeena in the first place. Before long, however, he became increasingly aware of Zeena's real nature, of her hypochondria, her "narrow-mindedness and ignorance." "Then she too fell silent"; and recalling his mother's growing taciturnity, Ethan began to wonder if Zeena were also turning "queer." "At times, looking at Zeena's shut face, he felt the chill of such forebodings." By the time of Mattie's arrival, nevertheless, the estrangement of the couple was so complete that even with his love for Mattie suffusing his whole being, the mere mention of her name was sufficient to seal him in silence: "Ethan, a moment earlier, had felt himself on the brink of eloquence; but the mention of Zeena had paralyzed him."

COMPLEX INTERRELATIONS

Just as the house stands in symbolic opposition to the out-of-doors, so too the bedroom of Zeena and Ethan is the direct symbolic counterpart of the shadows of the Norway spruces. For at the end of Chapter II and the beginning of Chapter III, it is evident that the bedroom represents for Ethan his suffocating marital commitment to Zeena and his frustrating separation from Mattie. The bedroom, moreover, is the scene of the first incident "of open anger between the couple in their sad seven years together"; in this scene, the obvious antithesis to that of the lovers under the spruces, "their thoughts seemed to dart at each other like serpents shooting venom." Thus Ethan's desertion of his bed that same night and his retirement to the study below foreshadow his subsequent resolution to desert Zeena and run away with Mattie.

Ethan's hope of an escape from his bondage to Zeena, however, soon withers in the harsh light of day and reality: "The inexorable facts closed in on him like prison-warders handcuffing a convict. There was no way out—none. He was a prisoner for life. . . ." Returning now to the narrative framework, one notes that this image of the shackles reappears in the description of Ethan's lameness "checking each step like the jerk of a chain." His very attempt to escape through suicide, in fact, had only doubled the bonds of his captivity; for his crippled body only objectifies the warped state of his soul, now chained to the ruins of a tragic marriage and even more tragic love. It is no wonder, then, that Ethan appears to the engineer to be already "dead" and "in hell." Here there is no hope or meaningfulness at all—only the endurance of despair.

In retrospect it may be seen more clearly how intricately *Ethan Frome* is structured. In spite of the obvious formal distinction between the framework and the narrator's "vision," the two parts are nevertheless complexly interrelated; the account of Ethan's tragic love, in fact, is so thoroughly informed by the sensibility and imagination of its narrator that the story can be adequately analyzed only in terms of that relationship. Since the narrator has had to imagine almost the whole of Ethan's history and the most important traits of his character as well, in many respects, inevitably, the sensibilities of the two are indistinguishable.

It seems to me, therefore, that it would be much more reasonable to judge the novel in terms of the special character of the narrator's mind—his predilection for poetic, symbolic design and an abstract ideal of human nature—rather than in terms of psychological realism. For even within the formal structure and statement of the work, Ethan and Mattie and Zeena are much more imagined than real characters. One may take issue, perhaps, with the rightness of the narrator's vision but certainly not with his right—or the right of the author—to imagine it as his peculiar sensibility dictates. Respecting this "vision," finally, and its metaphorical construction, it may be well to recall what [novelist and long-time Wharton friend] Henry James wrote in defense of [his novella] *Daisy Miller*, that his "supposedly typical little figure was of course pure poetry, and had never been anything else."

The Theme of Naturalism

Helge Normann Nilsen

Naturalism was a literary movement that began in the late nineteenth century and extended itself into twentieth-century literature in a variety of ways. Influenced by the evolutionary theories of Charles Darwin, naturalism in literature depicted humans as victims at the hands of a hostile environment over which they have little or no control. In this essay, Helge Normann Nilsen, who lectures in English at the University of Trondheim in Norway, analyzes the extent to which the naturalistic worldview influenced both Edith Wharton and the overall structural and thematic thrust of *Ethan Frome*.

Both as a theory about reality and a literary practice, naturalism presents a materialistic and agnostic world view. As a philosophic doctrine it has been defined

> as the theory that the whole of the universe or of experience may be accounted for by a method like that of the physical sciences, and with recourse only to the current conceptions of physical and natural science; more specifically, that mental and moral processes may be reduced to the themes and categories of the natural sciences. It is best defined negatively as that which excludes everything distinctly spiritual or transcendental.

In other words, nothing exists but physical matter, movement and change without human meaning or end. Life itself is a chance product of the environment. The world, society, human beings, events; all can be explained in terms of material causes and conditions. Mechanistic determinism reigns, and the various kinds of social and moral conditioning that people are subject to are also a type of observable, determining forces.

The fiction of Edith Wharton is strongly colored by this world view. Her friend Egerton Winthrop introduced her at

Reprinted from Helge Normann Nilsen, "Naturalism in Edith Wharton's *Ethan Frome*," in *Performances in American Literature and Culture: Essays in Honor of Professor Orm Overland on His Sixtieth Birthday*, edited by Vidar Pedersen and Zeljka Svrjuga (Bergen, Norway: University of Bergen, 1995), by permission of the author. (References in the original have been omitted in this reprint.)

an early age to the thinkers whose works lay behind the naturalistic movement in literature. In this way she was introduced to

> the extraordinary world of Darwin and [English philosopher Herbert] Spencer, [English biologist Thomas] Huxley and [German biologist and philosopher Ernst] Haeckel. It was to Winthrop that she owed such understanding as she reached not only of the theory of evolution, but of the naturalist theory of the implacable power of the environment. Those fictional figures of hers who struggle pathetically and unsuccessfully against their stifling surroundings are belated offspring of the tutelage of Egerton Winthrop.

Later in her life Wharton visited churches and seemed to harbor religious sentiments:

> Those who had known her from old in tight possession of another doctrine, her brain swept clear of any cobwebs of mystification, in all the severity of her rationality—it was natural for them, marking these signs of change, to take them as betokening a slipping and sliding of her assurance that could only end in one way, at one point of rest.

The point of rest refers to Christianity, but [early Wharton biographer Percy] Lubbock insists that Wharton, in spite of having tender sentiments towards churches, never abandoned her naturalistic world view.

In her fiction she takes mechanistic determinism as her starting point and sets about demonstrating how the theory works in practice, what happens to her characters and the reasons why. Her approach is in keeping with the theory of the experimental novel developed by [French novelist and social critic Emile] Zola, the father of naturalism. Here, the novelist works like a scientist, introducing characters into a given physical environment and "observing" what happens to them. Under the chosen conditions a set of outcomes, usually tragic, are shown to be inevitable. In "Ethan Frome" Wharton may concern herself more with the presence and influence of nature than Zola would have done, but the method is the same. Given their time, place and circumstances, the characters in the novella cannot avoid their fate. In classic naturalistic, pessimistic fashion they become victims who cannot control their own lives. The plot itself is deterministic, and effect follows cause in an unbroken downward curve ending in disaster. The characters may have a free will in principle and be differently equipped for the struggle for survival, but they are ultimately subject to the workings of outside forces and not free agents in any meaningful sense.

NATURALISM AND *ETHAN FROME*

In addition to determinism it has been suggested that three features are essential to a definition of American literary naturalism of the late nineteenth and early twentieth centuries. These are *survival, violence* and *taboo*. The Darwinian survival struggle is represented in the muted but fierce battle of wills between Ethan and his semi-invalid wife Zeena. As for violence, it does not occur on the personal level, but is very much present in nature. Impersonal forces and blind chance are violent in themselves, as seen in the upheavals of nature and climate and in the catastrophic sledding accident at the end. Taboos are broken, though not in the most typical naturalistic way of describing the squalid and seamy sides of life. Wharton's coolly disillusioned presentation of nature and life is a different but quite as shocking violation of the Victorian taboo on atheism and agnosticism.

Carefully observing cause and effect, the author assembles the evidence and builds her case. Three forces dominate: the natural, the economic and the social, and Wharton demonstrates how her characters have no hope of rising above their circumstances. The first chapter opens with a paragraph that sets the tone for the whole story, presenting the overwhelming impact of nature in winter:

> The village lay under two feet of snow, with drifts at the windy corners. In a sky of iron Orion flashed his cold fires. The moon had set, but the night was so transparent that the white house-fronts between the elms looked gray against the snow, clumps of bushes made black stains on it, and the basement windows of the church sent shafts of yellow light far across the endless undulations.

The harsh climate oppresses people and limits their options severely. The universe itself is neutral or hostile towards human concerns, as suggested by the imagery of iron, ice and cold. In relation to this, the activities and lives of mere human beings become insignificant and pathetic. The destinies of the main characters illustrate perfectly Wharton's somber vision. Moreover, her determinism embraces all of the characters, also those who might be regarded as winners in the Darwinian struggle. The young Denis Eady is the son of a successful grocer and stands to inherit a thriving business, but the story also contains a glimpse of him as an old man. In the end he, like everyone else, will succumb to old age and death. The author's emphasis is never on freedom or choice, but always on limitations and constraints.

ZEENA AS A NATURALIST CHARACTER

In a tale such as this the plot demonstrates the inexorable march of cause and effect. It originates in the struggle for self-preservation of Zeena when she realizes that she may lose her husband to Mattie, a young woman and relative who lives with them and helps with the housework. This plot, driven by Zeena's indomitable will, is hinted at in the beginning when we are told that she is the one who has suggested that Mattie should go to church dances. Zeena's motive here is that the girl thus might meet a man and no longer be around to tempt Ethan.

Zeena's strategy for getting rid of her rival and keeping her provider is skillful and decisive. Her arguments appear to be reasonable and well-founded when she maintains that Mattie is too inexperienced to do the housework properly. She also points out that she cannot trust the girl to take care of her because she may marry Denis Eady and leave the Frome farm. Zeena is a hypochondriac who uses her illnesses, real or imagined, to further her own interests. That her sickness is largely imaginary becomes evident after Ethan's and Mattie's accident, when she turns out to be stronger than one would have expected. From the start she has made up her mind about Mattie and has arranged for a new hired girl to take her place. The two others, who fall in love with each other, are taken by surprise and are outmaneuvered.

Zeena's meanness is very real, but Wharton makes it clear that she cannot really be blamed for securing her own interests, given her situation, with no other means of support except her husband. This is in keeping with the general situation for women at the time. The alternatives for Zeena are unthinkable: destitution and charity. As for Mattie, she has to rely on the goodwill of relatives and ends up as an unpaid maid in Zeena Frome's household. Both women are victims of the traditional female role, which the story shows as another burden or determining force.

Wharton's dramatic irony is an important vehicle for the expression of her pessimism. When Zeena goes away to Bettsbridge to see a new doctor, the arrival of Mattie's replacement, the hired girl, is imminent, but Ethan and Mattie are blissfully unaware of this fact. The happy evening that the two spend together in the house is only a moment in a fool's paradise, serving to emphasize the tragedy that follows. The love between them is also frustrated because of Ethan's passivity, scruples and misplaced conscience. He is no match for Zeena and her scheme of pleading serious illness to gain her ends.

Throughout the story the author keeps contrasting Ethan's and Mattie's hopes for love and joy with the implacable forces arraigned against them. Together they appreciate the beauty of nature and enjoy walking home after a church dance. But the world around them is not very promising: "They stood together in the gloom of the spruces, an empty world glimmering about them wide and grey under the stars". Even more eloquently, the headstones in the little Frome graveyard mock Ethan's aspirations. They seem to tell him that his efforts are futile, that he will never get away from or manage to change his circumstances for the better. He is indeed trapped, like those who have gone before him.

In a similar way, Zeena herself assumes the proportions of an unavoidable fate blocking his way as she stands in the doorway, a forbidding presence for the two lovers arriving at the house this winter night:

> Against the dark background of the kitchen she stood up tall and angular, one hand drawing a quilted counterpane to her flat breast, while the other held a lamp. The light, on a level with her chin, drew out of the darkness her puckered throat and the projecting wristbone of the hand that clutched the quilt, and deepened fantastically the hollows and prominences of her high-boned face under its ring of crimping-pins.

The presence and influence of this deceptively frail woman are just as imposing as nature itself or the existing economic restraints. The ominous nature of her decisiveness is further underlined by the description of the kitchen, which seems like a cold vault, an abode of the dead. These references foreshadow the disastrous denouement of the tale. Wharton also emphasizes the ironic contrast between the beauty of nature and its very real menace to human well-being and happiness. The next day the winter morning is crystal clear, the sun is burning in a pure sky, and the shadows are dark and blue and "beyond the white and scintillating fields patches of far-off forest hung like smoke."

THE ECONOMIC AND SOCIAL STRUGGLE

The economic and social determinants are also fateful enough. Mattie has been left penniless after her father died a criminal and a bankrupt and her mother died of the shock and scandal. These events hint at the brutal economic forces at work in early American capitalist society. Mattie has also not received any education that could have enabled her to acquire a decent job. Similarly, Ethan and his mother have been victimized by socio-economic circumstances and illness. His father died in an accident and Ethan had to take over the Frome farm. He was made poor, however, by the fact that his father had become half-mad and had given away his money before he died. When a new railway was laid, the traffic on the road near the farm ceased and an unfortunate isolation was established. As a result, Ethan's mother became mentally disturbed and stopped talking altogether. When she was dying Ethan's cousin Zenobia, or Zeena, came to nurse her, and because of his own extreme loneliness caused by the isolation, Ethan appreciated Zeena's company and talk more than he would have done under normal circumstances. To avoid the total isolation he saw looming ahead during the coming winter months he made his fateful proposal of marriage to Zeena.

Later, Ethan had reflected that this would not have happened if his mother had died in the spring rather than in winter. Thus he also became a victim of chance, or ill luck. The marriage to Zeena turned out to be the main obstacle to the fulfillment of Ethan's plans and wishes. He wanted to move to a town and become an engineer, but Zeena's hypochondria and pride made her unwilling to live in a bigger place where she would not be noticed. At the same time it is suggested that she has valid reasons to seek security above all else. Life in a town would mean more opportunities and diversions for her husband, whereas she would have less status and power. In this, as in the problem with Mattie, Zeena knows where her interests lie and acts to secure them. In Starkfield, their small rural community, her many afflictions are admired by the other women, many of whom are also obsessed with illnesses and symptoms.

With Zeena away, Ethan and Mattie plan a happy evening together, and to begin with things go well. However, the cat disturbs them. It seems to represent Zeena in some way, and a fate that is bent on thwarting the two lovers' intentions. It leaps upon the table, upsetting its mistress' pickle dish so that it breaks, and then lies in her chair, watching the two lovers through narrowed eyes. Zeena herself is present in the spirit, so to speak, and Mattie begins to feel uncomfortable sitting in Zeena's chair a while later. At this moment, Ethan experiences an upsetting kind of vision, or image: "It was almost as if the other face, the face of the superceded woman, had obliterated that of the intruder."

After Zeena's return the battle of wills between the spouses is out in the open. Ethan is made furious by the resolute manner in which Zeena tells him about the impending arrival of the hired girl, and a quarrel ensues. Now the brutal, underlying realities of their relationship are revealed: "Through the obscurity which hid their faces their thoughts seemed to dart at each other like serpents shooting venom. Ethan was seized with horror of the scene and shame at his own share in it. It was as senseless and savage as a physical fight between two enemies in the darkness." In the elemental power struggle the beasts within bare their fangs, and there are echoes in this passage of naturalistic writers like [Jack] London and [Theodore] Dreiser and their interest in atavism, or regression under stress. In [Dreiser's] *Sister Carrie*, for example, Hurstwood is shocked by the icy reaction of his wife after she has learnt of his affair with Carrie and decides to divorce him. She takes both his property and his children, in her eye there is a "cold, steely determination" and she looks at him like "a pythoness in humour." Similarly, Ethan Frome regards his wife with a new fear and distrust, a creature that has been transformed into "a mysterious alien presence, an evil energy secreted from the long years of silent brooding."

The naturalistic knowledge and awareness of the hazards of working-class life are also present in the tale. Gloomily, Ethan contemplates the probable fate of a Mattie left alone to fend for herself:

> Despair seized him at the thought of her setting out alone to renew the weary quest for work. In the only place where she was known she was surrounded by indifference or animosity; and what chance had she, inexperienced and untrained, among the million bread-seekers of the cities? There came back to him miserable tales he had heard at Worcester, and the faces of girls whose lives had begun as hopefully as Mattie's.

This passage reminds a reader familiar with American naturalism of, for example, a work such as Stephen Crane's *Maggie: A Girl of the Streets* and its heroine's descent into prostitution and death. These are the realities of Ethan's world that he has been spared from thinking about till now. But he is aware of them and is determined to save Mattie from such horrors. He thinks of going West with Mattie and starting a new life, but the circumstances are simply too unfavorable. The trap is closing on him, the situation that most Wharton protagonists find themselves in eventually. The author compares him to a handcuffed convict, a man facing imprisonment for life. In view of this it is curious that a prominent Wharton critic should argue that the author "believed that men and women were largely responsible for their own happiness or despair, and that the gods who are supposed to make mischief among us are but figments of our collective imagination." Judging from "Ethan Frome" and other fictions by Wharton the opposite seems to be the case.

NATURALISTIC GLOOM

The desperate Ethan, casting about for a way out, decides to ask Mr. Hale, owner of the saw-mill, for a fifty-dollar advance on his lumber delivery. He plans to say that he needs the money because of Zeena's poor health. However, on his way he meets Mrs. Hale, who speaks kindly to him, and his resolve weakens. His New England scruples put a stop to his plans, and he feels that he is unable either to deceive the Hales or abandon Zeena to her fate. Reversing himself, he has to face reality. He is a poor man whose desertion might spell the end for his wife, and he does not have it in his heart to deceive old friends and neighbors who have always trusted him. The bitter irony is that his conscience, which is supposed to be a force for good, indirectly leads to his and Mattie's suicide pact at the end of the story and the final, tragic fate that befalls all of the three main characters. Mattie is reduced to a cripple, and Ethan is permanently injured after the fateful collision between their sled and a big elm tree that they believed would end their lives. The bitter ending has occasioned a criticism to the effect that the story is cruel. Wharton is charged with a "limitation of heart" which amounts to a "literary and moral deficiency of her work." But this amounts to blaming the author for the unhappy events that she has described. Her narrative is said to be deficient because it does not make the disastrous fates of its characters meaningful in some larger, perhaps metaphysical sense. But Wharton's point is precisely that no meaningful context is to be found, though this does not mean that her tale lacks such a dimension. It emerges in its awareness of the inequalities and injustices of socio-economic circumstances.

The ultimate irony of "Ethan Frome" is that the two unhappy lovers do not even succeed in escaping through death, but live on in a far more miserable state than ever before. Mrs. Hale utters the last words of the novella, suggesting that the three would be better off dead than alive, and this thought is entirely in keeping with the tone of the story. For the Fromes, and many others in similar circumstances at this period in American history, there can be no happiness or fulfillment in life. The naturalistic gloom is unrelieved. At the same time "Ethan Frome" is in itself a powerful protest against the prevailing socio-economic conditions of the times. It is a protest regarded as futile, but made despite everything. It is as if Wharton is saying that even if man is a helpless victim, one must yet protest and take a stand against the injustice and indifference of society and the universe.

Symbols Emphasize the Theme of Repression

R. Baird Shuman

R. Baird Shuman sees the strength of Ethan Frome *in the novel's rich symbolism, which Wharton uses especially well to communicate the hopes of the characters, their sexual repression, and the tensions between them. R. Baird Shuman is an emeritus professor of English at the University of Illinois at Urbana-Champaign, and he has written widely on American fiction and drama.*

There is probably no more pervasive single element in *Ethan Frome* than the symbolism. [Blake] Nevius and other writers have pointed out specific examples in which the landscape and the Frome dwelling are clearly related to the action of the story and to the development of characters within it. However, other symbolic elements have not been fully explored and these should be noted, because they are central to the work on a psycho-sexual level, and this level is very important to the novel because of the underlying sexual tensions which motivate its three central characters. Through the use of carefully chosen symbols, Wharton consistently emphasizes problems which are basic to the central action, and she also gives a very strong clue regarding the basis of Zeena Frome's hypochondria.

THE SYMBOLISM OF THE ELM TREE

One of the most notable symbols in *Ethan Frome* is the symbol of the elm tree into which Ethan and Mattie crash their sled during their ill-fated suicide attempt. It is evident that this tree might have been used by Wharton, either with conscious intent or subconsciously, as a phallic symbol. Note that the reader is told of the tree long before the suicide attempt is made and is thus prepared for what is later to happen. However, such ad-

Excerpted from R. Baird Shuman, "The Continued Popularity of *Ethan Frome*," *Revue des Langues Vivantes*, vol. 37, no. 3 (1971). Reprinted by permission of the author. (Footnotes in the original have been omitted in this reprint.)

vanced preparation is not entirely necessary; enough is said of the elm just before the accident to convince the reader of the danger it presents to anyone sledding down the slope which it partially obstructs. Mattie, speaking to Ethan about the elm, says, "Ned Hale and Ruth Varnum came just as *near* running into the big elm at the bottom. We were all sure they were killed. . . . Wouldn't it have been too awful?" Read on a symbolic level, and in light of the fact that later in the narrative the reader is told that Ethan had seen Ned Hale and Ruth Varnum kissing under the Varnum spruces, there is a clear indication that the elm stands as a representation of sexual temptation, that it draws to it those whose resistance is weak enough that they might violate the puritanical moral codes of a small New England community. Ned and Ruth, though tempted by love, are not pressed to the point that they violate the community mores. But Ethan and Mattie, though their love has not transgressed these mores in any physical sense, cannot long resist their physical natures and will soon be sufficiently dominated by these natures to violate the established codes.

Physical reality is hard and relentless; Wharton, in her introduction, warns the reader that it is with this "harsh and beautiful land" that she will concern herself. The harsh moral structures of this land prevent Ethan and Mattie from finding fulfilment for their love, and even the fulfillment of a death together is denied them. They collide head-on with the symbolic tree, and are doomed to a life of unbearable agony, both physical and mental. [Critic] Marilyn J. Lyde notes that in *Ethan Frome* ". . . there is no element of justice in the catastrophe. This is explained by the fact that Wharton was writing with the explicit purpose of counteracting the New England literary tradition of sweetness and light." The means which Ethan and Mattie chose for their suicide would lead a sensitive reader to expect some symbolic shadings to be apparent. These shadings are quite evident both in the fact of what the tree itself represents and in the fact that Ethan and Mattie run into it on a borrowed sled, on a sled which technically they have no right to, any more than Ethan technically has a right to Mattie's love, nor she to his.

A Barren House, a Mocking Graveyard, and Passionate Red

There is, throughout the novel, an emphasis upon the barrenness of the Fromes' lives and surroundings. The graveyard is constantly, mockingly in the background. Very early in the novel, the reader is told that Ethan has had to take down the "L" from his house, and Wharton, in a lengthy paragraph, tells that the "L" in a New England house is the center of all life, the hearth-stone of the dwelling. Zeena, presumably, is barren, and her barrenness pervades the atmosphere of the house and is constantly in direct contrast to Mattie's vitality. The illusion of barrenness is supported by such statements as "Zeena always went to bed as soon as she had had her supper, and the shutterless windows of the house were dark." And the statement which immediately follows this one is directly applicable to Ethan: "A dead cucumber-vine dangled from the porch like the crape streamer tied to the door for a death." The Freudian [relating to pyschoanalyst Sigmund Freud] overtones of the shutterless windows and of the dead cucumber-vine are clearly apparent. Death surrounds Ethan; the graveyard is a constant reminder of death's inevitability; and even as he looks ahead, there is no hope. He is the last of the Fromes. The future of his family, the hope of continuance, have been killed by his marriage to Zeena. Mattie presents a momentary hope of something wholesome and satisfying, but Ethan knows that she is what might have been, not what might ultimately be.

Although Mattie is not overly strong, she appears strong in contrast to Zeena. The reader is told that she has gained a great deal of strength during her year at Starkfield. She is often described in terms of the strong color red and its variations: "Mattie came forward, unwinding her wraps, the colour of the cherry scarf in her fresh lips and cheeks," ". . . through her hair she [Mattie] had run a streak of crimson ribbon." "Her [Mattie's] cheeks burned redder." "She [Mattie] looked so small and pinched, in her poor dress, with the red scarf wound about her." However, before Ethan's passion for Mattie had developed, she was sallow; and when she is described in terms of color, the color is more moderate: "You were as pretty as a picture in that pink hat." Red is also used symbolically in relation to the sun: "The sunrise burned red in a pure sky." "Now, in the bright morning air, her [Mattie's] face was still before him. It was part of the sun's red and of the pure glitter of the snow." This use of "red" and "pure" in the same sentence would seem almost to provide an element of mockery, for Mattie is the pure, the virginal figure, but the red heat of passion is intruding upon her life and is leading her irresistibly into a hopeless situation.

A RED PICKLE DISH AND A WOMAN'S HYPOCHONDRIA

Perhaps the most telling symbolic element in *Ethan Frome* is the cherished pickle dish which Zeena received as a wedding gift and has never used. When Zeena goes to Bettsbridge and leaves Mattie and Ethan alone overnight, Mattie takes this pickle dish from its accustomed place and uses it for its intended purpose. The cat, used symbolically throughout this part of the book to represent Zeena's inescapable presence, knocks the dish to the floor, and it is smashed. Zeena, almost immediately upon her return, discovers what has happened to the dish and blames Mattie for having used it. For the first time in the book, Zeena shows true emotion. "Her voice broke, and two small tears hung on her lashless lids and ran slowly down her cheeks."

This is a major tragedy for Zeena as Wharton presents the episode. The question, of course, arises of why this particular incident should be given such play. The smashing of the dish is not used as a pretext for sending Mattie away; Zeena has already reached the decision to do this. The incident might have been used as a turning point in the action of the novel, but it occurs after any turning point with which it might be directly associated. It is not used for characterization, because the characterization has been achieved as fully as it is to be by this point. However, on a symbolic level, is serves as explanation for Zeena's hypochondria and insecurity. The dish was a wedding gift and this, in itself, is significant. The fact that is was red and that is was a *pickle* dish adds to the sexual connotations which it might possess as a symbol. And the fact that Zeena cries because it is broken would point to the fact that Zeena is bemoaning her lost virginity and that her hypochondria is attributable to her fear of her husband's, and perhaps her own, animal nature. Zeena finds that her marriage has placed her in conflict with the codes which her New England upbringing instilled in her; her inhibitions have become so great that she is made pathological by them. Zeena is a pitiable woman. For one reason or another, she has never been able to find fulfillment. Her life is barren. Her future is dark. She reacted well to the responsibility of caring for Ethan's mother, because it was necessary to Zeena that she be needed. But with the death of Ethan's mother, there was a gap in Zeena's life. This gap might have been filled had she had children, but she was denied this satisfaction. Hence, her concern turned inward and her hypochondria, which apparently had moderated when she began caring for Ethan's mother, returned in full force.

To an extent, Zeena was rewarded for the suffering which she endured during the first seven years of her marriage when Mattie and Ethan were injured and needed Zeena to look after them. Zeena—like Ethan—is strongly masochistic throughout the novel. Her hypochondria provided her with masochistic satisfaction, just as her leaving Ethan and Mattie alone for the night did. But when she could become the martyred servant of the sharp-tongued wretch which Mattie became after the accident, her masochistic satisfaction found its greatest fulfilment. She could simultaneously feel that she was needed, that she was morally superior, and that she had been sinned against but had had the humanity to be forgiving.

NEW ENGLAND PURITANISM AND THE NOVEL

One critic has written that "Wharton conceived of the novel as an organism, the germ or controlling principle of which was character." Certainly the character of Zenobia Frome represented a controlling principle in the novel at hand, for in this character, Wharton represents in a single person the generalized, warped manifestation of New England puritanism in its most unwholesome extremes.

[Literary critic] Alfred Kazin has quoted Edith Wharton as saying that "Life is the saddest thing next to death." Yet in *Ethan Frome* life has become much sadder than death. Starkfield, the name of which sounds funereal, is a cemetery for those who are still physically alive. There is not "much difference between the Fromes up at the farm and the Fromes down in the graveyard; 'cept that down there they're all quiet, and the women have got to hold their tongues.". . .

Regardless of considerable adverse criticism, *Ethan Frome* remains a monument in the Edith Wharton canon. It is probably valid to say that it is the Edith Wharton novel which has been most read. . . . It retains a freshness in dealing with the problem of the marriage triangle from a relatively impersonal viewpoint. Nature and life and moral codes move steadily forth, drawing with them such as Ethan and Mattie. Wharton does not sentimentalize; indeed, she cannot sentimentalize if she is to achieve her end of producing a work which will counter the sweetness and light in which other novelists had steeped New England.

Shame's Dominion over Ethan Frome

Lev Raphael

In the book from which this section is excerpted, *Edith Wharton's Prisoners of Shame: A New Perspective on Her Neglected Fiction*, Lev Raphael illustrates the corrosive effect of shame over the lives of Wharton's characters. *Ethan Frome* the novel and Ethan Frome the character are no exception to this trend in Wharton's fiction. For Raphael, shame paralyzes not only Ethan, but its power and presence guide the lives of Mattie and Zeena as well, and in turn undermines all human possibility and potential. Lev Raphael's many books include the comic mystery *The Edith Wharton Murders*. He escaped academia in 1988 to write full-time and is the Book Critic for National Public Radio's *The Todd Mundt Show* and "Mysteries" columnist for the *Detroit Free Press*.

The narrator of *Ethan Frome*, on first observing Frome at Starkfield, is struck by Frome's "lameness checking each step like the jerk of a chain." Ethan Frome is chained to an even darker fate than Lily [Bart, the main character in Wharton's *The House of Mirth*], because he doesn't escape into death, yet his story too is one of disappointment, failure, powerlessness and shame—for him and in lesser ways for Mattie Silver and even his wife Zeena. The physical burden is matched by an emotional chain that constantly pulls Ethan short, that silences him, that constricts his life: shame over a lifetime of disappointments, culminating in being trapped ("most of the smart ones get away" from Starkfield), and over his deep inadequacies as a man. In *Ethan Frome*, shame becomes more and more potent a force as the novella progresses and its conflicts intensify.*

*Gershen Kaufman defines shame as "being seen in a painfully diminished sense." His seminal work "Shame, The Power of Caring" (Rochester, VT: Shenkman Books, 3rd edition, 1992) first appeared in 1980. He is so widely quoted that his work is even referred to by Alicia Silverstone's character in the movie *Clueless* when she talks about a "shame spiral," a term Kaufman introduced in his book.

Excerpted from Lev Raphael, *Edith Wharton's Prisoners of Shame: A New Perspective on Her Neglected Fiction* (New York: St. Martin's Press, 1991). Copyright © 1991 by Lev Raphael. Reprinted by permission of the author.

SILENCE AND SHAME IN THE CHARACTER OF ETHAN FROME

Kaufman notes that "the affective source of silence is shame, which is the affect that causes the self to hide. Shame itself is an impediment to speech." In the narrator's first extended contact with Frome, he reflects that Frome "seemed a part of the mute melancholy landscape, an incarnation of its frozen woe, with all that was warm and sentient in him fast bound below the surface...." Living in Starkfield, "silence had deepened about him year by year." We gain our first glimpses below that surface of silence watching Frome interact with the narrator, who is visiting Starkfield on an engineering job. Frome finds "a volume of popular science" that the narrator left behind, and with "a queer note of resentment in his voice" says the book is full of things he knows nothing about: "He was evidently surprised and slightly aggrieved at his own ignorance." For the narrator, these comments point up "the contrast... between his outer situation and his inner needs." Frome's "old veil of reticence" is a mask for the bitter life of disappointment. And even in a town where people have suffered enough to feel "indifferent" to others' troubles, Frome is seen as having "had his plate full up with [sickness and trouble] ever since the very first helping."

In the narrative built up about Frome, we learn of the early roots of his shame in disappointment. Though he had gone to a technical college for a year and been interested in physics, the death of his father "and the misfortunes following it" ended the possibility of study, and through that, escape from the constricting life of Starkfield. Unlike Lily Bart, Ethan Frome has no personal gifts or talents that can offer even the fantasy of a better life. His life of isolation changes, however, when Mattie Silver comes to stay with him and his wife.

MATTIE SILVER AND THE STRUGGLE AGAINST SHAME

Mattie... is the daughter of a cousin of Zeena's, whose misfortune has "indentured her" to the Fromes. Mattie's father "had inflamed his clan with mingled sentiments of envy and admiration" by a successful move to Connecticut, marriage and business ventures. But he mishandled money that relatives had given him, all of which was revealed after his death. The shameful disclosure killed his wife, and left Mattie a victim. "Her nearest relations... ungrudgingly acquitted themselves of the Christian duty of returning good for evil by giving [her] all the advice at their disposal." Zeena only took Mattie in because her doctor said she needed help around the house: "The clan instantly saw the chance of exacting a compensation from Mattie." Like Lily, Mattie is proof of someone else's beneficence, and her "liberation" is a kind of imprisonment, since she has to "pay" for her father's success, *and* his failure.

For Frome, Mattie's youth and enthusiasm offer him a pathway out of isolation. She is someone he can share his observations and thoughts with: "He could show her things and tell her things...." He also enjoys her "admiration for his learning"—she can make him feel happy and proud. Yet because of her new importance in his life, she is also a source of shame. Waiting to take her home from a squaredance in town, he is struck by not feeling special. Through a window he sees, "two or three gestures, which, in his fatuity, he had thought she kept for him... the sight made him unhappy." Even more painfully, he wonders "how he could ever have thought his dull talk interested her. To him, who was never gay but in her presence, her gaiety seemed plain proof of *indifference*" [my emphasis]. When she is leaving the dance,

> [a] wave of *shyness* pulled him back into the dark angle of the wall, and he stood there *in silence* instead of making his presence known to her. It had been one of the wonders of their intercourse that from the first, she, the quicker, finer, more expressive, *instead of crushing him by the contrast, had given him something of her own ease and freedom*; but now he felt as *heavy* and *loutish* as in his student days, when he had tried to "jolly" the Worcester girls at a picnic [my emphases].

Frome is "by nature grave and inarticulate [and] admired recklessness and gaiety in others"; one of Mattie's great gifts is to ease Frome's shame.... Wharton's intuitive understanding of shame is clear here; of course someone stiff and shy like Ethan would be struck by the contrast between himself and someone natural and free, and that invidious comparison would potentially be the source of shame. So much depends on her—and Frome attaches "a fantastic importance to every change in her look and tone."...

The night Ethan picks Mattie up at the dance, he is jealous of young, well-off Denis Eady, who had danced with Mattie. Later, thinking about Mattie and Denis, he will feel "ashamed of the storm of jealousy in his breast. It seemed unworthy of the girl that his thoughts of her should be so violent." Now, he is relieved when Mattie resists riding with Denis, but then Mattie's "indifference was the more chilling after the flush of joy into which she had plunged him by dismissing Denis Eady." Their idyllic walk home, "as if they were floating on a summer stream," ends with a grim reality: withered, censorious Zeena is waiting for him, and he goes up to their bedroom "with *lowered head*" [my emphasis]. Shame is certainly a key element of his relationship with Zeena, the cousin who came to nurse his mother, and who stayed after Mrs Frome died. Unlike Mattie, she arouses little that is positive in Ethan. Zeena's "efficiency shamed and dazzled him" and he keenly felt a "magnified . . . sense of what he owed her." Zeena's own shame helps trap him in Starkfield, which they had originally agreed to leave:

> she had let her husband see from the first that life on an iso-
> lated farm was not what she had expected when she mar-
> ried. . . . She chose to look down on Starkfield, but she could
> not have lived in a place which looked down on her. Even
> Bettsbridge or Shadd's Falls would not have been sufficiently
> aware of her, and in the greater cities which attracted Ethan
> she would have suffered a complete loss of identity.

Her feelings are thus clearly much more than . . . a "disinclina-tion to accept any change." Her power over Ethan manifests it-self in a critical silence, hinting at "suspicions and resentments impossible to guess." Still, though vaguely threatened by Zeena, he is not reduced to *complete* powerlessness: "There had never been anything in her that one could appeal to; but as long as he could ignore and command he had remained indifferent."

The balance between them changes when Zeena goes off for more doctor's advice and Ethan and Mattie spend some time together alone—their first such occasion, which is both festive and furtive. Ethan is "suffocated with the sense of well-being" coming in from his hard day's work, for dinner, but when Zeena comes up in their conversation, Mattie feels "the contagion of his embarrassment" and she flushes. The next day he feels intoxicated "to find . . . magic in his clumsy words," but he makes Mattie blush when he mentions hav-ing seen engaged friends of hers kissing: "now he felt as if her blush had set a flaming guard about her. He supposed it was his natural awkwardness that made him feel so."

Zeena's return with the diagnosis of "complications"—which confers morbid "distinction . . . in the neighbourhood"—precip-itates the first fight between Ethan and herself "in their seven sad years together." Zeena claims that she will need full-time help around the house that Mattie cannot supply, and bursts out that she would have been ashamed to admit to the doctor that her husband begrudged her the help, that she lost her health nursing his mother, and her family said he "couldn't do no less than marry" Zeena in the circumstances. Ethan explodes, and is "seized with horror at the scene and shame at his own share in it." Zeena taunts him with the possibility she might end up in a poorhouse, as other Fromes have done, and then Ethan's big lie is exposed. He had clumsily said he couldn't drive her to her train because he was going to get a payment for lumber from Andrew Hale. When he tried to get that unprecedented advance from Hale, Hale flushed, leaving Ethan "embarrassed." Shame kept him from pleading an emergency: since he had struggled to become solvent after his father's death, "he did not want Andrew Hale, or any one else in Starkfield, to think he was going under again." Frome naturally responds with anger when Hale asks if he is in financial trouble, because he of course feels further exposed.

Now, facing Zeena, Ethan blushes and stammers, trying to explain that there was no money coming in, and he is devastated when his wife announces she has hired a girl and that Mattie *must* go: he is "seized with the despairing sense of his helplessness." Ethan tries to shame Zeena into keeping Mattie, pointing out that people will frown on her kicking out a poor, friendless girl, but Zeena is adamant, leaving Ethan "suddenly weak and powerless"—and enraged:

> All the long misery of his baffled past, of his youth of failure, hardship and vain effort, rose up in his soul in bitterness and seemed to take shape before him in the woman who at every turn had barred his way. She had taken everything else from him; and now she meant to take the one thing that made up for all the others.

Ethan is so distraught that he blurts out to Mattie that she has to leave, and then feels "overcome with shame at his lack of self-control in flinging the news at her so brutally". The grim evening ends with Zeena's discovery that her prized pickle dish, a never-used wedding present, was broken during her absence when Mattie and Ethan were having dinner, and that Ethan had tried to hide the breakage. Glad that Mattie—with whom she compares so poorly—is leaving, Zeena's joy turns to profound sorrow at the destruction of the one treasure in her miserable life.

ETHAN'S ENTRAPMENT IN SHAME

Ethan longs for escape with Mattie to the West—but he hasn't enough money: "The inexorable facts closed in on him like prison-warders handcuffing a convict. There was no way out—none. He was a prisoner for life, and now his one ray of light was to be extinguished." In a way like Lily, "the passion of rebellion" breaks out in him and he plans to ask Andrew Hale for money to pay for Zeena's new hired girl (though the money would really be for his "escape"). After all, Hale knows Ethan's money troubles well enough for Ethan "to renew his appeal *without too much loss of pride*" [my emphasis]. On the brink of making this request, however, unexpected sympathy from Mrs. Hale turns Ethan away, with "the blood in his face." Having been accustomed to think people "were either indifferent to his troubles, or disposed to think [them] natural," he is warmed by her compassionate "You've had an awful mean time, Ethan Frome.". . . How can he dishonestly take money from the Hales when they sympathize with the way life has cheated him?

Still, Ethan's "manhood was humbled by the part he was compelled to play . . . as a helpless spectator at Mattie's banishment." When she later weepingly wishes she were dead, Ethan will feel ashamed too. Taking Mattie away, they stop at the pond where they first realized at a picnic that they loved each other; it is a "shy secret spot, full of the same *dumb melancholy* that Ethan felt in his heart" [my emphasis]. Their blissful reprieve of sledding turns into an attempted mutual suicide, but as in so many other things, Ethan fails to pull it off, and he and Mattie are left crippled and even more dependent on Zeena. Ethan is so ashamed of what his life has come to that no stranger sets "foot in [his] house for over twenty years."

All this, of course, is the *vision* of the narrator, and Frome is "the man he might become if the reassuring appurtenances of busy, active, professional, adult mobility were taken from him." The life of silence and constriction Ethan Frome leads is indeed a nightmare, but I see this as a nightmare in which shame has reduced human possibilities and even human speech to an almost unbearable minimum. Ethan's fantasies of being buried next to Mattie, his "warm sense of continuance and stability" at the sight of the family graveyard, is a longing not for passivity but for *release* from the crushing weight of a lifetime of humiliating failure and disappointment.

The Theme of Illicit Love

Alfred Kazin

In this perceptive overview of Edith Wharton's life, the society in which she lived, and the novel *Ethan Frome*, Alfred Kazin compares the facts of Wharton's own life–a disastrous marriage, her adult experience of New England, and the emotionally repressed environment in which she was reared—to the tragic dimensions of her best-known work. Literary critic Kazin argues that Wharton's treatment of illicit love punishes the lovers for their moral failings. Alfred Kazin's many works include *On Native Grounds: An Interpretation of Modern American Prose Literature* and *An American Procession.*

The story of poor Ethan Frome, chained to his tyrannically "invalid" wife, Zeena, on a miserable New England farm, unable to escape with his true love, Mattie Silver, except in a bungled effort at double suicide that leaves them both horribly crippled for life, has long been an American classic. (It was first published in 1911.) In its spare, chilling re-creation of rural isolation, hardscrabble poverty, and wintry landscape—forces that enclose and doom the already pitiful lovers—*Ethan Frome* overwhelms the reader as a drama of irresistible necessity. Although there is something mechanical and too obvious about the device framing the story—we are supposed to be getting at it through the eyes of a visitor to Starkfield, who is picking up the details from neighbors—we easily overlook this under the spell of genuine tragedy. No reader can escape the emotional force of *Ethan Frome,* the heartbreak of what the great New England poet Robert Frost, working the same regional cry of frustration, called "finalities besides the grave."

EDITH WHARTON AND NEW YORK HIGH SOCIETY

This most somberly New England of rural tales was composed in the rue de Varenne, in the heart of Paris's aristocratic Faubourg St. Germain, by a wealthy, patrician, extremely conservative American. She had originally begun the "nouvelle," as she always called it, as an exercise in French. The simple story and simple characters seemed to lend themselves to an exercise in a foreign language.

In spite of her subject, Wharton was far from being a New England regional novelist, such as Mary Wilkins and Sarah Orne Jewett; there were a dozen others "doing New England" at the time, and Wharton thought their minor efforts soft-minded. Born Edith Newbold Jones on East 21st Street in 1862, she felt that she represented patrician old New York during the Gilded Age against the "invaders," who represented nothing but money. She was contemptuous of what New York (and America generally) was becoming. With the wealth she inherited from family real estate, plus the royalties she accumulated from regularly publishing a novel almost every year, she lived grandly in France after giving up her great estate, The Mount, in Lenox, Massachusetts.

For all this wealth and consciousness of position, Edith Wharton was a rebel against the restrictions of her set and her early upbringing. In a day when even the wealthiest young women were not permitted access to advanced education, she had had to bring herself up intellectually. And that she certainly did. It was unheard of for a lady of her class to become a novelist, especially a social novelist with the kind of keen, acidulous sense of society's absurdity and duplicity that Edith Wharton had raked over so lightly but unmistakably in her novel of 1905, *The House of Mirth.*

A BAD MARRIAGE AND ILLICIT PASSION

To add to her extremely bitter sense of frustration and intellectual isolation in "good society," Edith Newbold Jones had been married off at twenty-three to a neurasthenic, idle, eventually unstable sportsman and bon vivant, Edward Wharton. "Teddy" Wharton was "vocationless," like Edith's own father. He did not share his wife's intellectual and literary tastes. He seems to have become increasingly depressed as his wife attained literary fame; to his wife's vexation, he began to demand a share of her considerable earnings, this even as he confessed being unfaithful to her.

Edith Wharton was among the first in her expatriate society to own a "strong and commodious motor car." She felt privileged enough to sail for Europe with six servants and her pet dogs. She seemed very haughty indeed to those outside her select circle of literary luminaries and French aristocrats. [Novelist] Henry James was regularly whisked about in her "motor," and her intimates included [art critic] Bernard Berenson, art historian Kenneth Clark, and international lawyer Walter Berry. But her struggle to establish herself as a literary artist and intellectual on equal terms with her European familiars, plus her increasing desperation at having to live with the inactive, difficult, envious Teddy Wharton, had fostered extraordinary bitterness. It was by no means dispelled in her one, great illicit love affair with expatriate American journalist Morton Fullerton.

Illicit passion, as it used to be practiced in deadly secrecy, was a preeminent horror to those American friends of Edith Wharton's, descendants of the Puritans, who regarded themselves as lawgivers to the rest of America. Harvard's Charles Eliot Norton, a professor of the fine arts and the very incarnation of the genteel tradition, loftily informed Edith Wharton that "no great work of literature has ever been based on illicit passion." Although she was not the creative equal of [Gustave] Flaubert in *Madame Bovary* or [Leo] Tolstoy in *Anna Karenina*, the risk and ultimate tragedy of the illicit became the steady concern of her imagination. What is most noteworthy about her handling of the illicit in novels such as *The House of Mirth* and *The Age of Innocence* is that extramarital passion, while a considerable temptation, is never squarely met. This avoidance gives Wharton's approach, for all its stylistic keenness and brilliance of observation, an unmistakable tone of melancholy. A sense of abiding frustration hangs over her every idea of love, always manifesting itself despite the superb expressiveness of her style, the wit, even acerbity with which she disparaged society in *The House of Mirth*, *The Custom of the Country*, and *The Age of Innocence*, and in many of her glitteringly expert short stories.

If Edith Wharton was not the equal of her great friend Henry James, if she lacked his high vision and avidity in pursuing a theme to the last morsel of personal consciousness, she was above all a consummate professional. In turning her jaundiced view of love and marriage on the hide-bound New England farm folk of *Ethan Frome*, she was able, in the most gripping way, to project her dark view of marriage onto a class and its customs that were far removed from her socially.

EDITH WHARTON AND NEW ENGLAND LIFE

What, it might have been asked when the book came out in 1911, did this grande dame living in such high style up at The Mount (be it ever so sporadic, her "real" life being in France) know of the general life that really went on, day after day, in the hard-pressed existence of the village she so significantly named Starkfield? How much did she know about farmers and storekeepers always on the verge of economic catastrophe, whom her greater familiarity with aristocratic Europe disposed her to think of as peasants? In her foreword to the novel, Wharton spoke all too summarily of "my figures" as "simple," described them as "but half-emerged from the soil, and scarcely more articulate." Just as she originally thought her own limited mastery of French rich enough for such simple people, even in *Ethan Frome*, which she finally wrote in English, she is condescending toward the character Harman Gow, when she states that he "developed the tale as far as his mental and moral reach permitted."

There is no doubt that the overwhelming, painful starkness of *Ethan Frome* derives in part from Edith Wharton's extreme consciousness of class. Farm and village life in New England a century ago did seem socially hopeless. As it says in the novel, "Most of the smart ones get away." It is a matter of record that in the years following the Civil War, three-fifths of Connecticut, three-quarters of Vermont, and nearly two-thirds of New Hampshire and Maine declined in population. Historian Arthur M. Schlesinger, Sr., describes "Cellar holes chocked with lilac and woodbine, tumbledown buildings, scrubby orchards, pastures bristling with new forest growths, perhaps a lone rosebush—these mute, pathetic memorials of once busy farming communities attested the reversal of a familiar historic process, with civilization retreating before the advancing wilderness."

It was this decline that made New England picturesque, gave rise to the school of local color that Wharton disparaged. Although life below The Mount made her mindful of "the short and simple annals of the poor," what fascinated her about Ethan, Zeena, and Mattie was as always a chance to display her underlying sense of fatality. She symbolized this feeling in the dreariness of winter, the bareness of Ethan's farmhouse, the insufficiency of his sawmill (his principal crop being lumber), the meanness of an existence that allows Zeena to tell Mattie that a just-emptied medicine bottle can be used for pickles.

EDITH WHARTON AND LOVE'S FATALISM

The sure, powerful, even menacing strokes with which Wharton described the poverty and dull routine, the claustrophobia of village life, the stupefying lack of communication between husband and wife in the same house–all these factors give special force to *Ethan Frome*. Yet *Ethan Frome* is not so much a social novel in the author's usual high style as it is a driving, seemingly irrefutable treatment of her favorite theme: illicit love. For love to really be love, it must be forbidden, it must fail, it must carry the doomed lovers down with it. It is Wharton's addiction to this theme, with hardly any sympathy for her characters (with the exception of Ethan himself, who is accorded all the hallmarks possible of strength and sensitivity, but who is unable to use them), that lends such grimness to her plot and evokes this unswervingly depressing scene. The poverty of the lovers (in every sense) is rendered pitilessly. The horrible Zeena, because she is so horrible, is the most convincing character: She alone seems to explain the impasse that is Wharton's inspiration. Whenever Zeena dashes Ethan's hopes, whenever the wintry lonely atmosphere brings out one excruciating depth more of Ethan's brooding sorrow, we are caught— caught up in the author's seemingly irresistible sense of nemesis. Yet the handling of these desperate matters is hypnotically professional. The author can make us believe that Ethan's and Mattie's defeat, leading them to seek death (and, obviously, sexual fulfillment) in an ecstatic sleigh ride down the great hill, is their only way out. And of course this must end in a terrible crippling of both lovers, a death-in-life.

Such is Edith Wharton's belief in the irreversibility of circumstances *and* character: Certain things are fixed forever. Despite her sympathy for the lovers, she is in an old-fashioned American way the strictest of moralists. Although there is nothing to live for but love, love really to be love must be illicit, and so end in mutilation and lifelong pain.

Wharton would have us believe that all Ethan and Mattie needed to get away was fifty dollars. Lacking the money, they had to kill themselves. Although marvelous stage business–*Ethan Frome*, in its spareness and headlong drive toward disaster, made an equally hard-hitting play in the 1930s—it is a bit too dramatic. What drives the lovers to seek death is not the lack of fifty dollars, but Wharton's favorite obsession. Love *must* transgress conventional morality, but it cannot. It consequently becomes a chimera, an impossibility, a cheat. "Life," the author once said, "is the saddest thing, next to death."

Some such compulsiveness is behind the barren scene, the strictness, even the mercilessness with which *Ethan Frome* unfolds. Technically the book is positively "exemplary" in the way it enforces a descending pattern of events. From the opening of Ethan's story, with its raising of his hopes, to the crushing final scene—a now recovered Zeena presiding forever over the crippled, totally defeated lovers— we are made aware that things are "just so." Not otherwise. Not ever!

CHAPTER 3

Characters in *Ethan Frome*

The Male Narrator's View Controls the Reader's Perspective

Susan Goodman

Susan Goodman provocatively argues that the narrator's "vision" of Ethan Frome's story is flawed because it gives only Ethan's—not Mattie's or Zeena's—point of view. Wharton deliberately contrives the narrator's shortcomings, Goodman claims, so that the reader cannot fully trust the narrator. Therefore, readers must fill in the gaps of understanding that this complex triangle of characters necessarily creates. If we endeavor to fill in these gaps, a very different picture of Zeena and Mattie emerges, Goodman concludes. Susan Goodman teaches English at the University of Delaware, has published widely on Edith Wharton, and recently published a biography of American novelist Ellen Glasgow.

Before *Ethan Frome*, as [early Wharton critic] Blake Nevius states, "the narrators employed in Edith Wharton's early stories are *always men*." It seems significant, therefore, that Wharton's next novel, *The Reef* (1912), is the story of a woman's growing consciousness, told primarily from her point of view, that undermines men's symbolic constructs of female behavior. The change in narrative perspective suggests that the writing of *Ethan Frome* helped to prepare its author to assume and sustain a voice closer to her own.

Wharton's unnamed narrator is an example of what she saw herself becoming if she could not find new ways of using old plots. He is a self she sheds, for as [historian] Carroll Smith-Rosenberg observes, "the act of adopting another's language can be tricky and costly, even if one does so with a self-conscious, ironic intent." Arguing that male plots are in-

Excerpted from Susan Goodman, *Edith Wharton's Women: Friends and Rivals.* Copyright © 1990 by the University Press of New England. Reprinted by permission of the University Press of New England, Hanover, N.H.

adequate for describing a female writer's experience, [critic] Joanna Russ asks who ever read a short story about a girl going off into the wilderness alone, killing a bear, and returning a woman. Wharton is grappling with the same issue in *Ethan Frome*. Her narrator sees what he has been primed to see culturally and literarily. By undercutting his authority and reliability, she dissociates herself from his error: telling the wrong story. As the ghostly landscape of the novel suggests, she saw that road ending in frozen creativity.

The tale the narrator tells of two women and one man is a story that Wharton told all of her life, but unlike her, he does not challenge its convention, nor does he highlight the falsity of categorizing and stereotyping the rivals. To him, the phrase "two women and one man" is explanation enough for why the Frome farmhouse is not a home. If Wharton had seen only as much as her narrator saw, she would have lost her individual identity as a writer in much the same way that Frome becomes a part of "the mute melancholy landscape, an incarnation of its frozen woe."

IDENTIFYING WITH ETHAN

The narrator's identification with Ethan determines his point of view. From Ethan he envisions a tale of triangular passion. It is, however, only one of many possible ways of telling the story; for example, Mattie Silver could speak for all poor relations, who have no choice but to suffer a cousin's querulous tongue and the advances of her husband. Wharton goes to excessive length, or, one could say, to excessive ellipsis, to make this point. Forced to take shelter from a blizzard in the Frome farmhouse, the narrator informs us: "I found the clue to Ethan Frome, and began to put together this vision of his story. . . . .
. . . .
. . . ." The extended fade-out emphasizes that what follows is just what the narrator has said, a vision of Ethan Frome; and it grows from the narrator's initial response to him: "the sight pulled me up sharp. Even then he was the most striking figure in Starkfield, though he was but the ruin of a man." When the narrator crosses the threshold of the Frome farmhouse, he fleshes out this original fragment, which might be titled "The Ruin of a Striking Man."

Ethan is the narrator's creation just as surely as the narrator is Wharton's, and, in fact, Ethan the character appears to the narrator in much the same way that Wharton describes her characters intruding upon her consciousness: "I may be strolling about casually in my mind, and suddenly a character will start up, coming seemingly from nowhere. Again, but more breathlessly, I watch; and presently the character draws nearer, and seems to become aware of me, and to feel the shy but desperate need to unfold his, or her tale." As she explains in her introduction, his function mirrors her own:

> Each of my chroniclers [Hamon Gow and Mrs. Ned Hale] contributes to the narrative *just so much as he or she is capable of understanding* of what, to them, is a complicated and mysterious case; and only the narrator of the tale has scope enough to see it all, to resolve it back into simplicity, and to put it in its rightful place among his larger categories.

The narrator is not as reliable as the quotation first appears to suggest, for his "larger categories," in part Aristotelian [in the style of Greek philosopher Aristotle] and gender-bound, are not Wharton's.

SEEING BEYOND THE NARRATOR

Wharton believed that books that shed "a light on our moral experience" result from the author's ability to see beyond his or her characters. Above all, she valued—without questioning the concept—the "human significance" of the universal. The narrator, however, never sees beyond the personal, and he mistakes such superficial likenesses as an interest in popular science and joint sojourns in Florida for deeper similarities between himself and his subject. By describing the protagonist and the narrator as if they were puppets (Ethan's lameness checks each of his steps "like the jerk of a chain" and his observer is "pulled up sharp,") Wharton underscores her own distance from them.

In an allegorical reading of the novel, the narrator is a pilgrim, traveling to a critical junction. Like the speaker in the Robert Frost poem ["The Road Not Taken"], he must choose between two roads. One is known and leads to his desired destination, the Corbury power plant, but a blinding snowstorm has swallowed its track. If he is to reach his goal, if he is to be empowered, he must continue by forging a second, original path. Wharton articulated the narrator's challenge in *The Decoration Of Houses* (1898): "Originality," she said, anticipating [poet and critic] T. S. Eliot's "Tradition and the

Individual Talent" (1917), "lies not in discarding the necessary laws of thought, but in using them to express new intellectual conceptions."

Instead, the narrator chooses a road that leads into an in-
fertile and frozen landscape, past "an orchard of starved apple-
trees writhing over a hillside among outcroppings of slate
that nuzzled up through the snow like animals pushing out
their noses to breathe." This road ends at the Frome farmhouse, but like the road to Corbury Junction it too could
lead—as it did for Wharton—to an original story on familiar
lines. However, the formula of two women and one man dictates that the tragedy results from competition for Ethan.

ZEENA AND THE MEANING OF THE STORY'S "GAPS"

By calling attention to the limits of this vision, Wharton
manages to have her narrator tell an old story while suggesting a new one; for example, Ethan sees Mattie no more
clearly than when Zeena's "volubility was music in his
ears":

> She laughed at him for not knowing the simplest sickbed du-
> ties and told him to "go right along out" and leave her to see
> to things. The mere fact of obeying her orders, of feeling free
> to go about his business again and talk with other men, re-
> stored his shaken balance and magnified his sense of what
> he owed her. Her efficiency shamed and dazzled him.

By the novel's end this dynamo is transformed into a ghoul,
whose "pale opaque eyes" reveal nothing and reflect nothing. The reason is obvious: Ethan is more child than husband. Silent and remote, he offers her no choice but to endure like his mother, Endurance Frome. Not only has he
broken the promise to move to a larger city, but he has done
so on the pretext that there "she would have suffered a complete loss of identity." In passive retaliation, Zeena assumes
a new identity as a hypochondriac. She is like one of her
geraniums with the faded, yellow leaves that "pine away
when they ain't cared for." Whether her illnesses result from
a need for attention or from suppressed anger, they are
symptomatic of the Fromes' marriage, and in that sense
Ethan is also diseased.

Zeena's characterization makes one particularly aware of
what the narrator said at the beginning of his tale: "the
deeper meaning of the story was in the gaps." Wharton asks
the reader to fill them in. Despite the narrative point of view,
Zeena has a right to berate Mattie for breaking the red glass

pickle dish that was a present from her Philadelphia relatives: "You're a bad girl, Mattie Silver, and I always known it. It's the way your father begun, and I was warned of it when I took you, and tried to keep my things where you couldn't get at 'em—and now you've took from me the one I cared for most of all—." That neither the narrator nor her husband credits her point of view again shows Wharton's distance from them and her criticism of their shared perspective. Mattie and Ethan have shattered Zeena's heart as thoroughly as they have the dish; and although Wharton's choice of dish humorously puns on Mattie and Ethan's situation (they're in a pickle), sympathy must extend to Zeena, whose own romantic fantasy has materialized into hours of unappreciated drudgery. The narrative's masculine perspective excludes her story, which could be one of unbearable loneliness, emotional and economic deprivation, or, physical and psychological abuse.

Herself a realist and a realistic writer, Wharton knew the dangers of romantic notions and of romance plots obscuring the actual. Ethan's failure really belongs to his author, the narrator, who has not succeeded in characterizing either Mattie or Zeena in the round. The women's pairing throughout the story reinforces how little individuality they have in the narrator's mind. Mattie comes to the Frome house to help as Zeena came to care for Ethan's ailing mother seven years before. The women merge first in the narrator's imagination when he enters the Frome kitchen and then in the vision he attributed to Ethan: "She stood just as Zeena had stood, a lifted lamp in her hand, against the black background of the kitchen. She held the light at the same level, and it drew out with the same distinctness her slim young throat and the brown wrist no bigger than a child's." Wharton simultaneously exposes the distortion of Mattie's characterization and the self-serving nature of romantic visions by having Ethan's desire affect his perception, as before his eyes she becomes "taller, fuller, more womanly in shape and motion."

Although lovely, Mattie is possibly the most inarticulate heroine in American literature, and her name is indicative of her position and treatment in the Frome household. She is indeed, as Ethan notes, a "serviceable creature" either as Zeena's doormat or Ethan's dream lover; for example, when she responds to the sunset by saying, "'It looks just as if it was painted!' it seemed to Ethan that the art of definition could go no farther, and that words had at last been found to utter his secret soul." Ethan first sees Mattie as an extension of himself. Finally, they become one on that winter night's ride down Corbury Road when "[a]s they flew toward the tree . . . her blood seemed to be in his veins." In the narrator's telling, Ethan has been the author of this fiction; and as the quotation illustrates, it ends with the appropriation of Mattie's identity. . . .

Everyone on the Starkfield farm is a victim of the romantic plot's inadequacy for dealing with life's day-to-day plodding and day-to-day boredom. No rescuer will appear, and no fortunes will be reversed after Ethan wakes to the sound of Mattie making a noise "like a field mouse," "a small frightened *cheep*." The lovers' crippling shows the danger of cheap romantic fantasies: "The return to reality was as painful as the return to consciousness after taking anesthetic." Doomed to pass all of this life and the next in each other's company, Mattie, Zeena, and Ethan's predicament predates [French existentialist philosopher Jean-Paul] Sartre's vision of hell in his 1945 play *No Exit (Huis clos)*. In this way Wharton's stark realism triumphs over the narrator's tragic romanticism. Mattie's arms may encircle Ethan on that fateful ride just as Maggie Tulliver hugs her brother Tom, but she and Ethan are predestined to be torn apart. The fiction of their union cannot be sustained.

Ethan Expresses Wharton's Greatest Themes

Blake Nevius

Blake Nevius maintains that Ethan Frome is one of Wharton's finest creations. Through Ethan, the hopes, failings, and torments that characterize Wharton's greatest characters and fiction are powerfully expressed. Blake Nevius taught at the University of California at Berkeley for many years. His book *Edith Wharton: A Study of Her Fiction* was one of the first, and remains one of the best, studies of Wharton's fiction.

Although much has been made of this minor classic of our literature as a picture of New England life and a triumph of style and construction, its relation to Wharton's more characteristic and important stories has never been clearly established. *Ethan Frome* is not a "sport." It belongs to the main tradition of Wharton's fiction, and it has a value, independent of its subject and technique, in helping us to define that tradition. [Critic] Alfred Kazin has linked it to [Wharton's novel] *The House of Mirth* as a demonstration of the spiritual value of failure, but although this is a recurrent theme in Edith Wharton, particularly in the novels she wrote in the twenties, and is inescapable in the conclusion of *The House of Mirth*, it is no mean feat, I think, to reconcile it with the episode which forms the narrative framework of *Ethan Frome*. She was by no means convinced of its soundness, and it is possible, as I intend to suggest, that the spectacle of Ethan's prolonged and hopeless defeat, reinforced by the glimpses of his spiritual isolation, his scarred and twisted body, and his querulous, demanding womenfolk, is intended to convey quite the opposite of what Kazin finds in the story.

Excerpted from Blake Nevius, *Edith Wharton: A Study of Her Fiction* (Berkeley and Los Angeles: University of California Press, 1953). Copyright © 1953 The Regents of the University of California. Reprinted by permission of the publisher.

The final, lingering note of the story, it seems to me, is one of despair arising from the contemplation of spiritual waste. So emphatic is it that it drowns out the conventional notion of the value of suffering and defeat. Ethan himself sounds it just before his last, abortive effort to escape his destiny:

> Other possibilities had been in him, possibilities sacrificed, one by one, to Zeena's narrow-mindedness and ignorance. And what good had come of it? She was a hundred times bitterer and more discontented than when he had married her: the one pleasure left her was to inflict pain on him. All the healthy instincts of self-defence rose up in him against such waste. . . .

THE FUTILITY OF SELF-SACRIFICE

And taking Wharton's novels as a whole, that note swells into a refrain whose burden, as George Darrow in [Wharton's novel] *The Reef* formulates it, is "the monstrousness of useless sacrifices." Here is the ultimate result of that "immersion of the larger in the smaller nature which is one of the mysteries of the moral life." As a theme, the vanity of self-sacrifice is merged repeatedly with the primary theme of the limits of individual responsibility. A realization of "the monstrousness of useless sacrifices" encourages the characters' selfish, passional bent, which is curbed in turn by the puritanical assertion of responsibility. For Ethan as for most of Edith Wharton's protagonists who are confronted by the same alternatives . . . the inherited sense of duty is strong enough to conquer, but the victory leaves in its wake the sense of futility which self-sacrifice entails. Their moral transactions are such as to preclude a satisfactory balancing of accounts.

How and to what degree does the situation in *Ethan Frome* embody this conflict? No element in the characterization of Ethan is more carefully brought out than the suggestion of his useful, even heroic possibilities. He had longed to become an engineer, had acquired some technical training, and is still reading desultorily in the field when the narrator encounters him. This is one aspect of his personality. There is still another which helps explain why Edith Wharton, who was deeply drawn to nature, is predisposed to treat his case with the utmost sympathy: "He had always been more sensitive than people about him to the appeal of natural beauty. His unfinished studies had given form to this sensibility and even in his unhappiest moments field and sky spoke to him with a deep and powerful persuasion." Add to these qualities his superior gifts of kindness, generosity, and sociability, and his impressive physical appearance ("Even then he was the most striking figure in Starkfield, though he was but the ruin of a man"), and it is evident that Edith Wharton set about, as [Herman] Melville did with Ahab [in his novel *Moby-Dick*], to invest her rather unpromising human material with a tragic dignity.

ETHAN AND THE TRAGEDY OF LOST POTENTIAL

It is in view of his potentialities that Ethan's marriage to Zeena is a catastrophe. By the time Mattie Silver appears on the scene, he is only twenty-eight, but already trapped by circumstances and unable to extend the horizon of his future beyond the family graveyard. Mattie, once she has become the victim of Zeena's jealousy, offers a way out which Ethan is quick to follow. But immediately his plans are set afoot, things begin to close in on him again: farm and mill are mortgaged, he has no credit, and time is against him. Moreover, even in the heat of his resentment he cannot disregard Zeena's plight: "It was only by incessant labour and personal supervision that Ethan drew a meagre living from the land, and his wife, even if she were in better health than she imagined, could never carry such a burden alone." His rebellion dies out, but only to be rekindled the next morning as Mattie is about to leave. Suddenly it occurs to him that if he pleads Zeena's illness and the need of a servant, Andrew Hale may give him an advance on some lumber. He starts on foot for Starkfield, meets Mrs. Hale en route, is touched by her expression of sympathy ("You've had an awful mean time, Ethan Frome"), continues toward his rendezvous— and is suddenly pulled up short by the realization that he is planning to appeal to the Hales' sympathy to obtain money from them on false pretenses. It is the turning point of the action:

> With the sudden perception of the point to which his madness had carried him, the madness fell and he saw his life before him as it was. He was a poor man, the husband of a sickly woman, whom his desertion would leave alone and destitute; and even if he had the heart to desert her he could have done so only by deceiving two kindly people who had pitied him.

Although he is neatly hemmed in by circumstances, it is Ethan's own sense of responsibility that blocks the last avenue of escape and condemns him to a life of sterile expiation.

A REDUCTION OF LIFE'S POSSIBILITIES

In *Ethan Frome* all the themes I have mentioned are developed without the complexity that the more sophisticated characters and setting of [Wharton's novel] *The Fruit of the Tree* and . . . *The Reef* require; they are reduced to the barest statement of their possibilities. To a person of Ethan's limited experience and his capacity for straightforward judgments, the issues present themselves with the least ambiguity or encouragement to evasion; and in this, I believe, we have the measure of the subject's value for Wharton. As her characters approach her own sphere, their motives are disentangled with increasing difficulty from her own, and their actions are regulated by a closer censure; they become more complex and are apt to lose their way amid fine distinctions and tentative judgments. They are aware . . . of the impossibility of basing a decision upon absolutes. . . .

Ethan Frome is closer than any of her other characters to the source of the ideas that underlie Edith Wharton's ethical judgments. Puritanism has lost very little of its hold on that portion of the New England mind which he represents and its ideas have not been weakened, as they have in the more populous industrial and commercial centers, by two centuries of enlightenment based on what [dramatist and critic] Bernard Shaw called the Mercanto-Christian doctrine of morality. It is not surprising that many persons unacquainted with Edith Wharton's biography associate her— and not wholly on the strength of *Ethan Frome*—with Boston or with New England as a whole. Whatever the influences exerted by her New York origin and background and her long career abroad, it is the moral order of Ethan Frome's world that governs the view of reality in all her novels. . . .

THE TELLING OF ETHAN'S STORY

Ethan Frome marks a gain in artistry that was to be consolidated later in *The Reef* and *The Age of Innocence.* The first important work to appear after Edith Wharton had established her permanent residence abroad, it had been undertaken as an exercise in French to modernize her idioms, but had been abandoned after a few weeks. A sojourn at the Mount, some years later, had revived the story in her mind, and it had been written in Paris during the following winter. From the directness and simplicity of the style of the final version, one might suppose that it had been composed entirely in French and then translated, but it was in fact an independent growth from the original seed. She and [friend] Walter Berry had "talked the tale over page by page," and the results of their collaboration may be glimpsed in the fragment of a working version preserved among the manuscripts at Yale. Berry was a rigorous taskmaster. "With each book," Edith Wharton acknowledged gratefully, "he exacted a higher standard in economy of expression, in purity of language, in the avoidance of the hackneyed and precious." The stylistic restraint of the final version, unusual even for Wharton, may in part be a tribute to his discipline. How many revisions the tale underwent may never be known, but a comparison of the manuscript fragment with the corresponding portion of the printed text indicates that Edith Wharton worked hard to meet Berry's standards and to eliminate redundancies, circumlocutions, and ambiguous or misleading expressions, realizing that the language as well as the theme of *Ethan Frome* had to be treated "starkly and summarily."

WHARTON'S SYMPATHY FOR ETHAN

Enough has been said, by Wharton among others, about the technical resourcefulness brought into play by the peculiar difficulties of telling Ethan's story; but in view of the widespread feeling that the author's human sympathies were hobbled by her rationalism, it should be stressed that the best touches in the story are there because she felt her subject deeply enough to be able to charge it with conviction at every point. The details are few but impressive; they arise directly and easily, and always with the sharpest pertinence, from the significant grounds of character and situation; they are, as [critic] Percy Lubbock suggests, "the natural and sufficient channels of great emotion." Every reader will recall some of them: Mattie's tribute to the winter sunset—"It looks just as if it was painted"; Ethan's reluctance to have Mattie see him follow Zeena into their bedroom; the removal of Mattie's trunk; the watchful, sinister presence of Zeena's cat disturbing the intimacy of the lovers' evening together by appropriating her mistress' place at the table, breaking the pickle dish, and later setting Zeena's rocking chair in motion. Zeena may not be a sympathetic character, but there is a moment when she makes us forget everything but her wronged humanity. As she confronts the guilty lovers, holding the fragments of her beloved pickle dish, her face streaming with tears, we have a sudden and terrible glimpse of the starved emotional life that has made her what she is. The novelist's compassion can reach no further.

ETHAN AND THE NOVEL'S SYMBOLISM

Although it functioned generally at a mundane level, Edith Wharton's imagination could occasionally be roused to symbol-making activity by the conjunction of a theme and a setting both deeply cherished and understood. In *Ethan Frome* her theme is enhanced by every feature of the landscape: by the "orchard of starved apple-trees writhing over a hillside among outcroppings of slate," the crazily slanted headstones in the Frome graveyard, the truncated "L" of Ethan's farmhouse in which one saw "the image of his own shrunken body," but predominantly by the landscape as a whole, buried under snow, silent and incommunicative as the characters. The method looks ahead to [Wharton's novel] *Summer*, with its naturalistic symbol of the Mountain and its subtle accommodation of the human drama to the rhythm of the changing seasons; to the moment in *The Reef* when Darrow recalls his vision of Anna Summers advancing toward him slowly down an avenue of trees, now transformed in his imagination to the passing years, with the "light and shade of old memories and new hopes playing variously on her"; and to *Hudson River Bracketed*, [another Wharton novel] with its dominating symbol of the Willows, equated in Vance Weston's mind with the Past he is struggling to recapture in his first novel. Only in *Ethan Frome*, however, is the symbolism sustained by every element in the setting. It is the one occasion in her longer fiction when her imagination worked freely and without faltering in this extra dimension.

Ethan and Entrapment

Anja Salmi

Anja Salmi sees Ethan as the typical antihero of Wharton's fiction: He is incapable of action because of his moral sense of duty to others. The irony of this situation is that characters morally inferior to Ethan always triumph over him. What results is a hopeless sense of entrapment, much like a figure from Greek mythology. Anja Salmi is a Finnish academic, and the study from which this selection was excerpted was selected by Finland's Academy of Science and Letters for publication.

Ethan . . . is a Whartonian Andromeda, and the whole novelette starts with a chain image. But the first hardship entrapping all the characters is the New England winter. Harmon Gow, the narrator's informant and a former stage driver, tells the narrator why Ethan looks so old and "as if he was dead and in hell": "Guess he's been in Starkfield too many winters. Most of the smart ones get away." After spending one winter there, the narrator begins to understand what Harmon Gow means. After being exposed to the elements, he sees the six-month long winter personified as an enemy attacking the inhabitants and suppressing them:

> when the storms of February had pitched their white tents about the devoted village and the wild cavalry of March winds had charged down to their support; I began to understand why Starkfield emerged from its six months' siege like a starved garrison capitulating without quarter. Twenty years earlier the means of resistance must have been far fewer, and the enemy in command of almost all the lines of access between the beleaguered villages.

ETHAN'S LIFE OF SACRIFICE

The smart ones get away and Ethan, too, has tried. He wanted to be an engineer, and took a course in technology. He even went to Florida once, but first his father's illness,

Excerpted from Anja Salmi, *Andromeda and Pegasus: Treatment of the Themes of Entrapment and Escape in Edith Wharton's Novels* (Helsinki, Finland: Suomalainen Tiedeakatemia, 1991). Copyright © 1991 by Academia Scientiarum Fennica. Reprinted by permission of the publisher.

and then his mother's, caused him to return, to take care of the farm. Ethan marries Zeena, a relative come to the farm to help him nurse his mother, because he felt so lonely after both his parents had died. But the ultimate reason even for his marriage is winter, for Ethan "had often reflected that it would not have happened if his mother had died in spring instead of winter." The restlessness in him remained even after he got married. He had planned to sell the farm and move with Zeena to a bigger city, but he then "learned the impossibility of transplanting her. She chose to look down on Starkfield, but she could not have lived in a place which looked down on her." The flashbacks into Ethan's past reveal all this.

Ethan has been living in imprisonment on an isolated farm, with a bitter, querulous, sickly wife, for seven years when Mattie comes into his life. Mattie is a poor relative of Zeena's, whom Zeena has taken into their home to help, as Mattie is an orphan and has nowhere else to go. Mattie is young, warm, and gay; she is Ethan's soul mate, who brings joy to his life. Ethan realizes how different life would be with her, but he is entrapped in his marriage. Here we have the elements of the pattern that keeps recurring in Wharton's novels.

[Critic Blake] Nevius says: "In the antiromantic tradition, none of the love affairs in Edith Wharton's novels require interest or significance until one or both of the partners is married. Once she has her characters ensnared as a result of their sentimental miscalculation, she is able to introduce a second contingent theme [moral obligation, the first theme being 'the immersion of the larger in the smaller nature']." Wharton repeatedly creates a triangle of one man and two women. [Wharton critic Cynthia Griffin] Wolff calls the recurring pattern the use of the double heroine. The hero usually meets the wrong heroine first and often marries her, only to discover that he has made a mistake. He then starts pining for the second heroine, who is his soul mate. . . . Thus Wharton's couples are usually "like ghostly lovers of the Grecian Urn, forever pursuing without ever clasping each other."

CONTRASTING HEROINES

In *Ethan Frome*, the contrast between the two heroines is brought to extremity. Mattie's gaiety and admiration of Ethan is in sharp juxtaposition with Zeena's taciturnity and constant complaints. The looks of the two heroines are in utmost contrast. To accentuate this, Wharton creates a pair of scenes where Zeena and Mattie in turn open the door to Ethan, and he observes them from the threshold, a frequent vantage point in both this novel and others. First Zeena. Zeena is the monster of the story, the incarnation of reality to Ethan:

> Against the dark background of the kitchen she stood up tall and angular, one hand drawing a quilted counterpane to her flat breast, while the other hand held a lamp. The light, on a level with her chin, drew out of the darkness her puckered throat and the projecting wrist of the hand that clutched the quilt, and deepened fantastically the hollows and prominences of her high-boned face under its ring of crimping-pins. To Ethan, still in the rosy haze of his hour with Mattie, the sight came with the intense precision of the last dream before waking. He felt as if he had never before known what his wife looked like.
>
> She drew aside without speaking, and Mattie and Ethan passed into the kitchen, which had the deadly chill of a vault.

And Mattie the night after:

> She stood just as Zeena had stood, a lifted lamp in her hand, against the black background of the kitchen. She held the light at the same level, and it drew out with the same distinctness her slim young throat and the brown wrist no bigger than a child's. Then, striking upward, it threw a lustrous fleck on her lips, edged her eyes with velvet shade, and laid a milky whiteness above the black curve of her brows.... A bright fire glowed in the stove.

Zeena is connected with the extreme cold of the kitchen, even with death, giving the vision the tone of a ghost tale. Mattie is linked with a bright fire, increasing the contrast to the utmost. It is as if Ethan were seeing two possibilities of life. First, the desolate view of life as it now is, the wife being seen "under the X-ray of indifference," when there is no loving feeling to retouch the picture; this is followed by a dream vision of what life, at its best, could be.

Mattie is everything that Zeena is not—she is different. Different is the key word in Whartonian love affairs.... Zeena, e.g., "never changed her mind," but "the motions of [Mattie's] mind were as incalculable as the flit of a bird in the branches."

Color symbolism connected with Wharton's double heroines appears first in *Ethan Frome*.... On the night that Ethan and Mattie are alone in the house, Mattie has run a streak of

crimson ribbon through her hair and has laid the table carefully, putting Ethan's favorite pickles in a dish of gay red
glass. Red, the color of vitality and passion, is thus connected with Mattie, whereas everything about Zeena is grey
or colorless.

An element of jealousy is added to Ethan's feeling towards
Mattie. . . . Maliciously, Zeena—like a serpent shooting venom
—talks to Ethan about Mattie marrying a young man called
Denis Eady, and Ethan even sees them dancing together.

When Zeena notices Ethan's interest in Mattie, she orders
Mattie to leave. For one whole night Ethan tries to figure out
how to raise the money to go with Mattie and leave the farm
to Zeena, but it is all to no avail. Nobody would buy a poor
farm like theirs, Zeena would lack the strength to take care
of it alone, he and Mattie could not raise the money for tick-
ets to go West, let alone find work there. "The inexorable
facts closed in on him like prison-warders handcuffing a
convict. There was no way out—none. He was a prisoner for
life. . . ." Even the dead Fromes in the graveyard seemed to
mock him. "We never got away—how should you?"

ETHAN'S ATTEMPT TO ESCAPE BY DREAMING

Zeena's death would provide one means of escape, and the
thought crosses Ethan's mind several times. When the story
begins and Ethan is taking Mattie home from a dance, his
subconscious wish is reflected in his suspicions while they
are approaching the house: "A dead cucumbervine dangled
from the porch like the crape streamer tied to the door for a
death, and the thought flashed through Ethan's brain: 'If it
was there for Zeena—.'" Then, when they do not find the
key under the mat: "Another wild thought tore through him.
What if tramps had been there—what if. . . ." Finally, Zeena
comes and opens the door.

After her visit to the doctor's, Zeena tells Ethan she is "a
great deal sicker" than Ethan thinks and she has got "complications." Ethan knows that, in most cases, complications
are a death-warrant. The narrator comments: "Ethan's heart
was jerking to and fro between two extremities of feeling,
but for the moment compassion prevailed." It is not difficult
to conjecture what the other extremity is after Ethan has
spent a lovely evening with Mattie. . . .

Ethan is also entrapped emotionally, verbally, and by his
own character. He is not capable of taking concrete actions,

but escapes into a dreamworld—a typical Whartonian anti-hero.

The morning of Mattie's planned departure, Ethan comes up with one more way to raise money: to go to Hale, a carpenter to whom he delivers lumber and ask for an advance payment, using Zeena's illness as an excuse. But on his way to the Hales he meets Mrs. Hale, who expresses her sympathies towards Ethan for Zeena's ailment: "I always tell Mr. Hale I don't know what she'd a'done if she hadn't a'had you to look after her." Now the writer has trapped Ethan decisively: trapped him with his own ethics. He was prepared to deceive Zeena, but he cannot deceive himself. He was going

THE POWER TRIANGLE IN *ETHAN FROME*

By examining Ethan in terms of the kinds of triangular relationships that characterize so much of Wharton's fiction, Lois A. Cuddy contends that the reader can see how his notion of being in control of events is illusory and that power shifts dramatically throughout.

Ethan . . . has perceived himself in the role of decision-maker and, therefore, figure of some power. Yet, triangles also define his life and, consequently, in Wharton's scheme of things, his defeat. As an only child, he is called home from a technological college in order to work the farm for his mother and sick father. Because he has been forced into this position by values which make him responsible for his family's survival, he can pretend to himself that he is in control. After his father dies and his mother is sick, Zeena comes to the farm to create a new triangle, and Ethan deludes himself that he is in control of that situation because he still runs the farm. The same error in perception will dominate his relationship with Zeena and Mattie.

Always Ethan assumes that it is up to him, as the man, to make the choices that will determine life for the women as well as himself. However, a closer look at the text reveals that someone else is really always at the angle of power (sick father, mother, Zeena, Mattie, and finally Zeena and Mattie together) to make his life forever an agony of remorse and . . . a memory of "lost possibilities." It was, after all, Zeena's strength and Ethan's loneliness and guilt that led him into marrying her and perceiving himself as the providing male who offers a weak, vulnerable female a home.

Lois A. Cuddy, "Triangles of Defeat and Liberation: The Quest for Power in Edith Wharton's Fiction," *Perspectives on Contemporary Literature*, 1982.

to borrow money from these kind people on false pretenses, but he now realizes his moral standards won't allow it. He turns around, goes back home, and is ready to sacrifice Mattie. "I'm tied hand and foot, Matt. There isn't a thing I can do."

Wharton's trapped characters have to confront moral choices, but their decisions, though morally just, do not make them happy. To them happiness is an "enemy," "untamable," a wild winged creature impossible to catch. One can only wait and watch where it might land temporarily.

Mattie can think of no other escape but death. She suggests they kill themselves by coasting against a [tree]. They fail in their effort and remain crippled for the rest of their lives. Zeena takes Mattie back and Ethan is now trapped by isolation, cold, two querulous women who depend upon him, and his own lameness "checking each step like the jerk of a chain." Like his house and his garden, he, too, is mutilated.

It is of interest that no expression of guilt occurs in the minds of Ethan and Mattie throughout the whole story. . . .

Ethan feels no remorse. He only sees Zeena as his enemy: "their quarrel was as senseless and savage as a physical fight between two enemies in the darkness" and "There was a moment's pause in the struggle, as though the combatants were testing their weapons." To Ethan, Zeena is the embodiment of all his failures. She is made the most sinister female character in Wharton's novels: flat-chested; false teeth; lashless lids; asthmatic breathing; evil-minded; ailing; whining; always wearing a calico wrapper and a knitted shawl, with crimping-pins in her hair, a true monster. Mattie is Ethan's only hope of having wings and being able to escape from reality, if only in his dreams.

LEVELS OF BETRAYAL

Mattie, too, seems to have no compunctions for trying to steal Zeena's husband, even though Zeena gave her a home when she had nowhere to go.

But this means taking the story at its face value. If the coasting scene is taken as a metaphor for adultery, then the resulting physical lameness would have a deeper meaning of guilt that crippled the two for the rest of their lives. Seen in this light, the story operates on many levels. One example is the scene where Mattie takes down Zeena's precious pickle-dish to decorate the table for Ethan; the cat breaks the dish, and Ethan tries to glue it but fails. The episode can be seen as a metaphor for Mattie trying to break Zeena's marriage. When Zeena finds out about the dish, her reactions seem disproportionate for the dish itself. She wails to Mattie: "You've took from me the one I cared for most of all—" and breaks off into sobs. Or Zeena's cat breaking the pickle-dish that Mattie wanted to delight Ethan with, may be metaphorical for Zeena breaking the germinating love affair between Mattie and Ethan. The red pickle-dish that Zeena had got as a wedding-present but dared not use for fear of breaking it, while Mattie takes it down and uses it with Ethan, may be a metaphor for eroticism or sexuality. . . .

The reason for arranging the structure of the story in such an unusual way, placing in it a narrator who tells his vision of Ethan Frome, a story fancied by an outsider and not told by an omniscient narrator, may be Wharton's wish to distance herself from the tale and indicate that there is more to it than just the story told. There may even be a third layer, the autobiographical, under the literal and metaphorical. It has been suggested that Ethan is Wharton herself. According to [biographer R.W.B.] Lewis, *Ethan Frome* is "one of the most autobiographical stories ever written."

EDITH WHARTON AND ETHAN

One can easily find parallels between the writer and her hero. The way Ethan has to bury his dreams of becoming an engineer, Wharton, for so many years, had to bury her own dreams of writing. Ethan had to take down the adjunct of his house because he could not afford its upkeep. Wharton, in turn, for twelve years, had to reduce herself in her marriage, unable to pursue her calling.

Taking down the adjunct of the house, according to [critic Kenneth] Bernard, suggests "the sexual repression." It could also be a subtle metaphor for childlessness. Ethan has had to give up hope of offspring, as they have already been married for seven years. Barrenness of all kind is accentuated throughout the story: the landscape; the farm; even the name of the village, Starkfield, "connotes barrenness." Both of the above interpretations of the adjunct correlate with the writer's own life. She was childless, like Ethan and, according to Lewis, her sex life with Teddy Wharton was nonexistent.

Ethan feels isolated from the rest of the world: "We're kinder side-tracked here." Wharton, too, felt "side-tracked" from the cultural world and its literary circles when living in America. The barrenness, infertility and extreme cold may also refer to the cultural climate. . . . In the same way as Ethan was surrounded by the winter cold of Starkfield and dreamed of the warmth of Florida, Wharton suffered from the cold cultural atmosphere of America and longed for Europe.

It has also been suggested that the sickly Zeena is sickly Teddy Wharton and Mattie is Morton Fullerton, who, for a short period, brought warmth to Edith's life. Wolff points out that the novel was written towards the conclusion of the affair, and quotes Wharton about the matter: ". . . I have been warmed through and through never to grow quite cold again till the end. . . ." The same contrast of warmth and cold appears in the above statement as runs through the whole novelette with Mattie representing warmth and Zeena cold.

After some favorable reviews of *Ethan Frome*, Wharton writes to Fullerton: "They don't know *why* it's good, but it *is*." It sounds as if the two were sharing a secret. Besides, the initial letters of Ethan and Mattie, Edith and Morton cannot be mere coincidence. One would like to think that Wharton, to punish herself for her adultery, punishes her characters to heal herself and to purify her soul.

Zeena Represents the Nineteenth-Century Female Role

G.S. Rahi

Typically, it is not difficult to despise Zeena Frome and view her as a character who represents all that destroys Ethan and Mattie: petty narrow-mindedness; a spiteful, vindictive nature; and sickly repression. G.S. Rahi, however, places her character in a larger context and views her as representative of the predicament of women in the nineteenth century. In other words, her character is formed and deformed (as Mattie's is) by her sense of being trapped in a life that offers women few, if any, choices. Indian scholar G.S. Rahi's book *Edith Wharton: A Study of Her Ethos and Her Art* examines the extent to which Wharton's fiction questions and criticizes the ethics of the privileged society into which she was born.

Ethan Frome is one of the finest and most powerful illustrations of a theme to which Wharton returns again and again—that of trapped sensibility. Ethan marries Zeena out of a sense of gratitude for her having looked after his ailing mother. Ethan is thus a character who can be considered a member of a larger group in Wharton's fiction ... who commit similar sentimental errors and are trapped by their partners in a vicious grip from which they are too refined to break away. In *Ethan Frome* Zeena is, by and large, an unsympathetically conceived character. She is not only sickly and hypochondriac but she also revels in her sickness and uses her condition to blackmail and nag her husband. Wharton's treatment of Zeena's attitude towards her ailments is clearly ironic. Zeena is shown to have enough perversity to consider her ailments a mark of snobbery. When she declares: "I have

Excerpted from G.S. Rahi, *Edith Wharton: A Study of Her Ethos and Her Art* (Amritsar, India: Guru Nanak Dev University Press, 1983). Reprinted by permission of the publisher. (Endnotes in the original have been omitted in this reprint.)

complications" it is obvious that she means to be impressive. "Ethan knew the word for one of exceptional import. Almost everybody in the neighbourhood had 'troubles,' frankly localized and specified; but only the chosen had 'complications.'" Her ever-watchful person is represented in her absence by her cat who seems to be spying on the lovers and keeping a record for her mistress. It is this cat that breaks the pickle dish which causes so much suffering to the lovers. All the same, to see Zeena only as a tyrant would be to misread not only the tale but also the intention of Wharton. The life to which the Fromes have been condemned is not borne by Ethan alone; Zeena is also a sufferer. It will not be out of place to note that Ethan himself does not represent a living and vital principle. In fact, he is associated with death and graves. He visualizes Mattie not as a partner in love but as one in death. In his imagination the family graveyard presides. Much before he articulates his love for Mattie he thinks of her in terms of one who shall lie with him in the family graves. It is impossible to rest the blame of all this on Zeena. It has something to do with the very setting of life in Starkfield. Zeena is as much a victim of such a life. She is driven to become a shrivelled-up woman because her own aspirations are stowed away like the pickle dish. Wharton treats the scene of Zeena's discovery of the broken dish in such a powerful way that this trivial article assumes symbolic proportions and Zeena emerges a human being in her own pathetic intensity.

> "I'd like to know who done this," she said, looking sternly from Ethan to Mattie.
>
> There was no answer, and she continued in a trembling voice: "I went to get those powders I'd put away in father's old spectacle-case, top of the china-closet, where I keep the things I set store by, so's folks sha'n't meddle with them—" Her voice broke and two small tears hung on her lashless lids and ran slowly down her cheeks . . . and gathering up the bits of broken glass she went out of the room as if she carried a dead body. . . .

The tears, the trembling voice, the reverent handling of the broken pieces, her carrying these fragments as if they were a dead body—all these indicate a genuine feeling of loss and tragedy for Zeena. For her this pickle dish was as important as it was for Mattie to use it to please Ethan. The dish becomes a symbol of "the pleasure and passion that Ethan had sought and Zeena had thwarted in their marriage." It is true that Zeena had denied this pleasure to Ethan and herself—she had never used the dish—but there is no doubt about her attachment to it. That Mattie had sought to use it in her absence is recognized by Zeena as an attempt to usurp her place, and this is not something that she can take lightly. . . . Thus whatever may be the extenuating circumstances under which Ethan and Mattie seek to satisfy their souls with love, it cannot be disputed that such an attempt is a transgression of Zeena's right. That Zeena denies herself and Ethan the rightful affection and association cannot mitigate the fact that the lovers are her culprits. [Critic Blake] Nevius recognises that Wharton shows sympathy for Zeena at this point:

> Zeena may not be a sympathetic character, but there is a moment when she makes us forget everything but her wronged humanity. As she confronts the guilty lovers, holding fragments of her beloved pickle dish, her face streaming with tears, we have a sudden and terrible glimpse of the starved emotional life that has made her what she is.

THE SOCIAL CONTEXT OF ZEENA'S TRAPPED SENSIBILITY

It needs to be noted here that Nevius, despite his perceptiveness, does not go far enough in understanding the situation. While he observes that Zeena is herself wronged he does not see that it is not only Ethan who is trapped, but that Zeena also is locked in a situation that is not entirely of her own making. As in other novels of Wharton both of them are victims in a larger context. In fact Nevius is so near the truth that one regrets his not seeing the whole of it. Why is Zeena's life emotionally starved? Here it would be relevant to point out that like other characters in Wharton the protagonists of *Ethan Frome* are products of the culture of the society in which they live. It is a society that does not envisage any positive role for its women; they can be merely parasites. In such a situation Zeena does not fit at all. She has nothing to fall back on except her own neglected, and hence paradoxically over-attended, sickly body. [Critic] Elizabeth Ammons makes this point:

> For every well-trained professional woman like Wharton's surgical nurse in *The Fruit of the Tree*, Justine Brent, there were thousands of women shut away from corporate life and bitter about their static existences. At least Ethan meets fellow workers when he carts his timber to sale or goes in to town for supplies and mail. Farmers' women-folk normally went nowhere and did nothing but repeat identical tasks in

unvaried monotony. To make that isolation of women stark and to emphasize the sterility of life at the level of *Ethan Frome*, Wharton gives the couple no children; and the woman's name she chooses for bold-faced inscription on the only tombstone described in the family-plot is also instructive:"ENDURANCE." If Ethan's life is hard, and it is, woman's is harder yet; and it is sad but not surprising that isolated household women make man feel the full burden of their misery. He is their only connection with the outer world, the vast economic and social system that consigns them to solitary, monotonous domestic lives from which their only escape is madness or death.

In this connection it may be observed that the hypochondria of Zeena is only her own version of the equally destructive and negative preoccupations of the leisure women of [Wharton's novel] *The House of Mirth*. Bertha's pursuing lovers outside marriage, Judy's constant efforts to be the great hostess, Undine's preying upon her husband's energies to meet her expenses, and above all the infantile petulance of Bessy in *The Fruit of the Tree*, are expressions of the same alienation of woman which in the ultimate analysis is caused by the values of a society that denies them meaningful participation in the creative processes of life. Zeena's plight is worse only because of her social isolation as well.

What is true of Zeena is equally true of Mattie. While the contrast between the two women is certainly valid it is not the whole truth about their relationship. There is a certain similarity in their positions. Mattie has nowhere to go; no training prepared her to meet the exigencies of life. With a telling effect Wharton shows how Mattie becomes Zeena. The point made by Wharton should be clear: "As long as women are kept isolated and dependent, *Ethan Frome* implies, Mattie Silvers will become Zeena Fromes: frigid crippled wrecks of human beings whose pleasure in life derives from depriving others of theirs." The same applies to Ethan's mother, and Endurance, one of his ancestors. All of them are products of the ethos of their society.

"Neurosis Conquers All": Zeena's Triumph

Richard B. Hovey

Reacting against what he sees as overly specialized, excessive interpretations of *Ethan Frome*, Richard B. Hovey sees the work in more traditional terms: as a tragic clash between a generous, moral nature (Ethan) and a small-minded, scheming nature (Zeena). Hovey maintains that the real strength of the novel lies in the disturbingly real psychological portrait of neurosis that Wharton created with Zeena Frome. Richard B. Hovey, a professor of American literature at the University of Maryland, wrote *Hemingway: The Inward Terrain* (1968) and many other essays on American literature.

My premise is that the art of *Ethan Frome* is predominantly realistic. Another bias . . . is Freudianism of a sort. The starting point suggested is to look more closely at Zeena.

Rightly, her undefined sickliness is never a clear-cut disease; it is psychosomatic and hence more problematic to deal with. She is hypochondriac, for [psychoanalyst Sigmund] Freud one of the more recalcitrant manifestations of neurosis. Thus, the basic components of the husband-wife duel are set up. Zeena has her sickliness, to use as well as she can in her discontent. Ethan has his conscientiousness, his sense of being indebted to her at his time of greatest need. Much of the story depends on how these two forces interact. Whose weakness—or strength—will win out?

ZEENA'S MANIPULATION OF EVENTS

Zeena's debility brings Mattie to the Frome farm to help. Before Ethan and Mattie are fully aware of their shy love, Zeena is alerted. In her taciturn way she begins to manipulate to get rid of the girl. She catches Ethan furtively doing

Excerpted from R.B. Hovey, "*Ethan Frome*: A Controversy About Modernizing It," *American Literary Realism, 1870–1910*, vol. 19, no. 1 (Fall 1986); © 1986. Reprinted by permission of McFarland & Company, Inc., Publishers, Jefferson, N.C. 28640. (In-text page references to *Ethan Frome* in the original have been omitted in this reprint.)

some of Mattie's tasks, then makes him further uneasy by remarking that he has started to shave every morning. Hers is
a "way of letting things happen without seeming to remark
them, and then weeks afterward, in a casual phrase, revealing that she had all along taken her notes and made her in-
ferences." Her next tactic is to break the routine of placing
the key under the rug on one of those few evenings Mattie
attends a church social and Ethan goes to walk her home.
When she comes to let them in, Zeena's self-pitying misery
and unattractiveness, contrasted with the momentary cheer
Ethan and Mattie have shared, evidently make him feel
shame and malaise of conscience. Next, in announcing she
is going to another town to consult a new doctor, Zeena jabs
again: If Ethan is too busy, the hired man, Jotham Powell,
can drive her to the train station. Never suspecting her devi-
ousness and buoyed by anticipating that she can hardly return before the following evening, Ethan is led to tell his first
lie: "'I'd take you over myself, only I've got to collect the cash
for the lumber.'"

Wharton's exquisite rendering of the tryst during Zeena's
absence—the Puritan ethos intensifies its poignancy—and
the cat breaking the red-glass dish are too well known for
recounting. What might be marked about Ethan's attempt
the next day to buy glue (in hope of mending the dish before
Zeena returns) is that when, after galling delays, he does get
the item at a store, its proprietress, well-meaning Mrs.
Homans, calls to him as he turns for home, "'I hope Zeena
ain't broken anything she sets store by.'" We sense how
Ethan feels: as if this villager is somehow reading his secret.
Returned, he learns that Zeena has already gotten back. Circumstances and timing are kinder to her than to him.

The climactic chapter VII exemplifies Wharton's dra-
maturgic powers at their best. We discover how carefully
Zeena has planned, how decisive she has been, how swiftly
and surely she has acted. Ethan is no match for her cunning.
Dutifully calling her to supper, he gets "the consecrated formula": "'I don't feel as I could touch a morsel.'" Her
hypochondria is in fine fettle; she is "'a great deal sicker'"
than he supposes and has "'complications.'" Though such
news produces mixed feelings in Ethan, "for the moment
compassion prevailed." Looking for "a consolatory short
cut," he asks how reliable is this new doctor.

Zeena opens the attack: "'I didn't need to have anybody

tell me I was losing ground every day. Everybody but you could see it.'" Regularly now, she uses another formula as *the* authority to justify her claims: the-doctor-says. Ethan agrees she must follow the physician's orders. Whereupon he hears a "new note" in his wife's voice, "drily resolute." Her medical ally has instructed her that she must not do "'a single thing around the house'"—that she must get a hired girl. In fact, she already has the girl, who will arrive the next day and be paid an extra dollar weekly. The added expense dismays and angers Ethan: "'Did Dr. Buck tell you how I was to pay her wages?'"

In battle, Zeena is superb. Her every move counts. She goes for the jugular:

> "No, he didn't. For I'd 'a' been ashamed to tell *him* that you grudged me the money to get back my health, when I lost it nursing your mother!"

> "*You* lost your health nursing mother?"

> "Yes; and my folks told me at the time you couldn't do no less than marry me after—"

> "Zeena!"

Ethan is horrified and shamed by this exchange. Marriage has not made him a seasoned fighter. Zeena's arsenal is full: "'The doctor says it'll be my death if I go on slaving the way I've had to. He doesn't understand how I've stood it as long as I have.'" Next, she is at him with self-pity. When he promises he will do all the housework, she rejoins, "'Better send me over to the alms house and done with it.'" By declaring it is settled because he does not have the money, Ethan has dropped his guard. Zeena catches him in a lie, and deception is a skill he is not disciplined in. In "a level voice," she can now say:

> "I thought you were to get fifty dollars from Andrew Hale for that lumber."

> "Andrew Hale never pays under three months."

She sees his face redden. She nails him again: "'Why you told me yesterday you'd fixed it up with him to pay cash down. You said that was why you couldn't drive me over to the Flats.'" He stammers "'a misunderstanding.'" Quiet comes for a moment. Her change to seeming mildness so far misleads Ethan that he goes on about how much he can still do for both her and Mattie. Then: "Zeena, while he spoke, seemed to be following out some elaborate mental calculation. She emerged from it to say: 'There'll be Mattie's board less, anyhow.'" Ethan scarcely knows what has hit him. But he hears a sound he has never heard before—Zeena is laughing! "'You didn't suppose I was going to keep two girls, did you? No wonder you were scared of the expense.'"

A NOBLE NATURE'S DEFEAT AT THE HANDS OF A LESSER NATURE

Ethan is all but done for, though some further hammering awaits him as Zeena finishes him off. When he reminds her that Mattie is no hired girl but her own relative, Zeena is rock-hard. When he asks her what "'folks'll say'" if she ousts Mattie, Zeena, secure enough in the community's approval, can parry in a "smooth voice: 'I know well enough what they say of my having kep' her as long as I did.'" In fury, Ethan starts to strike his wife, then checks himself. He has no way to force Zeena to keep her own cousin. "Now she had mastered him and he abhorred her."

Triumphing, Zeena has more weapons. Again, timing and circumstance aid her. Ethan goes downstairs, Mattie promptly knows something is wrong, and they embrace and kiss passionately—for the first time. Desperate, he exclaims: "'You can't go, Matt! I won't let you! She's always had her way, but I mean to have mine now—.'" Suddenly Zeena is behind him. She has overheard. But, acting her usual self, she reports feeling "'a mite better.'" She eats well, looking "straight at Mattie" with "a faint smile." Then, in quest of her stomach powders on a high closet shelf, she finds the fragments of the pickle-dish where Ethan had hoped to conceal them. She faces the culprits with her query. Ethan, with his wretched ineptitude for duplicity, tells part of the truth, blaming the cat. How did that creature get into the closet? "'Chasin' mice, I guess'" is his explanation. Once more from Zeena comes "a small strange laugh." Mattie then tells the whole truth. Zeena thus gets the indisputable evidence she requires. Weeping for the loss of her treasure, she turns on Mattie: "'You're a bad girl, Mattie Silver, and I always known it. . . . If I'd 'a' listened to folks, you'd 'a' gone before now, and this wouldn't 'a' happened.'" In the ethos of Starkfield, "bad girl" may be translated as seducing adulteress, if not as whore. Mattie's fate is sealed. The rest is denouement, relentless in its logic. What action can Ethan take?

He was too young, too strong, too full of the sap of living to submit so easily to the destruction of his hopes. Must he wear out all his years at the side of a bitter querulous woman? Other possibilities had been in him, possibilities sacrificed, one by one, to Zeena's narrow-mindedness and ignorance. And what good has come of it? She was a hundred times bitterer and more discontented than when he had married her: the one pleasure, left her was to inflict pain on him. All the healthy instincts of self-defence rose up in him against such waste. . . .

Faced with no guilt-free exit, Ethan vacillates, fumbles among tangled alternatives. He has heard of one divorce that worked out well. So, maybe he can go out West with Mattie and turn over to Zeena the proceeds from the farm and sawmill? Money and the nitty-gritty of practicalities block this hope. The property, mortgaged to the limit, would not clear a thousand dollars; and even if Zeena's illness is a

OUR FIRST GLIMPSE OF ZEENA

In stark contrast to the brightness and vitality of Mattie, Zeena suddenly appears backlit in the doorway of the Frome household and quickly establishes her sullen yet dominating presence in Edith Wharton's Ethan Frome.

Then the door opened and he saw his wife.

Against the dark background of the kitchen she stood up tall and angular, one hand drawing a quilted counterpane to her flat breast, while the other held a lamp. The light, on a level with her chin, drew out of the darkness her puckered throat and the projecting wrist of the hand that clutched the quilt, and deepened fantastically the hollows and prominences of her highboned face under its ring of crimping-pins. To Ethan, still in the rosy haze of his hour with Mattie, the sight came with the intense precision of the last dream before waking. He felt as if he had never before known what his wife looked like.

She drew aside without speaking, and Mattie and Ethan passed into the kitchen, which had the deadly chill of a vault after the dry cold of the night.

"Guess you forgot about us, Zeena," Ethan joked, stamping the snow from his boots.

"No. I just felt so mean I couldn't sleep."

Mattie came forward, unwinding her wraps, the colour of the cherry scarf in her fresh lips and cheeks. "I'm so sorry, Zeena! Isn't there anything I can do?"

"No; there's nothing." Zeena turned away from her. "You might 'a' shook off that snow outside," she said to her husband.

sham, she could not manage alone. "Well, she could go back to her people, then, and see what they would do for her. It was the fate she was forcing on Mattie—why not let her try it herself?" Such appears fair-minded. Briefly Ethan's hopes rise when he runs across an advertisement: "Trips to the West: Reduced Rates." But he lacks cash for the fare; lacks enough collateral even to borrow ten dollars in Starkfield.

After a sleepless night, he and Mattie try to show hopefulness toward each other. Again, however, Zeena has acted swiftly. She has arranged that Mattie's departure will be so prompt that, in a single trip to the railroad station, Mattie will make the train for Stamford and the new girl will be picked up and brought back to the farm. Her plans working neatly, Zeena is feeling better, has "an air of unusual alertness and activity."

She walked out of the kitchen ahead of them and pausing in the hall raised the lamp at arm's-length, as if to light them up the stairs.

Ethan paused also, affecting to fumble for the peg on which he hung his coat and cap. The doors of the two bedrooms faced each other across the narrow upper landing, and to-night it was peculiarly repugnant to him that Mattie should see him follow Zeena.

"I guess I won't come up yet awhile," he said, turning as if to go back to the kitchen.

Zeena stopped short and looked at him. "For the land's sake—what you going to do down here?"

"I've got the mill accounts to go over."

She continued to stare at him, the flame of the unshaded lamp bringing out with microscopic cruelty the fretful lines of her face.

"At this time o' night? You'll ketch your death. The fire's out long ago."

Without answering he moved away toward the kitchen. As he did so his glance crossed Mattie's and he fancied that a fugitive warning gleamed through her lashes. The next moment they sank to her flushed cheeks and she began to mount the stairs ahead of Zeena.

"That's so. It *is* powerful cold down here," Ethan assented; and with lowered head he went up in his wife's wake, and followed her across the threshold of their room.

Edith Wharton's *Ethan Frome.*

Ethan feels passionately rebellious, but "his manhood . . . humbled by the part he was compelled to play." He must do something. One hope occurs to him. If he tells kind-hearted Andrew Hale that he needs the advance of a small sum on their lumber deal because Zeena's illness necessitates a servant, he may be able to ask "without too much loss of pride." If he reaches Hale's wife beforehand, success may be more nearly possible; "and with fifty dollars in his pocket nothing could keep him from Mattie." He does encounter Mrs. Hale first. Well-meaning, she probes Ethan's exposed nerve: She has heard the news of Zeena trying a new doctor. Then she adds:

> I don't know anybody round here's had more sickness than Zeena. I always tell Mr. Hale I don't know what she'd 'a' done if she hadn't 'a' had you to look after her; and I used to say the same thing 'bout your mother. You've had an awful mean time, Ethan Frome.

These remarks set Ethan's ethical dilemma. Most Stark-fielders were indifferent to or routinized his troubles; Mrs. Hale makes him feel less alienated in his misery. Maybe, in their compassion, the Hales will help? Then a second thought comes: "He was planning to take advantage of the Hales' sympathy to obtain money from them on false pretenses." His integrity gives him his answer: He cannot do it. A conscience and heart less tender would never have hesitated to mislead the Hales and abandon Zeena. Does his decision instance quixoticism, weakness, morbid scrupulousness, regression? [Wharton critic Cynthia Griffin] Wolff summarizes: "Ethan and Zeena have been brought together by their mutual commitment to the habits of care-taking; now they have become imprisoned by them." Wharton concludes the chapter: "even if he had had the heart to desert her [Zeena] he could have done so only by deceiving two kindly people who had pitied him." Duty wins, love loses.

Only a splinter of self-assertion remains to Ethan. Against Zeena's preference, he, not Jotham, will drive Mattie to the station. The couple is fully aware of the power of their love and of its hopelessness. On their way, they stop at the sled-track. To be sure, theirs is a romanticized love: They cannot part, ever; death is preferable. . . . Their attempted suicide by crashing into the big elm is familiar enough not to call for rehearsing. As everyone knows, these lovers win not the gift of death but the curse of death-in-life. . . .

THE IRONY OF ZEENA'S VICTORY

Yet there is a victory, human, recognizably Freudian, and of course Zeena's. Her deepest wishes are fulfilled. She wins her power struggle with Ethan. She defeats a rival who threatened her marriage. Her sadism is gratified: She can dominate and further hurt two other persons. Her masochism is appeased: She can inwardly praise herself for her dutiful martyrdom. She has earned social approval for taking in Mattie and devoting her life to the cripples. More needed now, she feels more important. Extra demands put upon her, she can no longer be quite so attentive to her own symptoms; so her hypochondria diminishes. With the blessings of her conscience, she can spend out her days punishing the sinners in her charge. Granted, the formula oversimplifies, but we might say of *Ethan Frome:* Neurosis conquers all.

Mattie Silver as the Female Intruder

Carol Wershoven

Most of Edith Wharton's novels deal with the monied, privileged world of New York high society—a world that seems a long way indeed from the barren setting of *Ethan Frome*. However, Carol Wershoven sees Mattie Silver as one of the most extreme examples of a character type present throughout much of Wharton's fiction: the female intruder. According to Wershoven, the female intruder in Wharton's novels is usually a braver, more vital woman, who enters a world to which she ultimately does not belong. In the course of Wharton's novels, the female intruder is usually destroyed by a hostile individual or society that is morally inferior to her. Carol Wershoven teaches at Palm Beach Community College. Besides her study of female characters in Wharton's fiction, she has published articles on Nathaniel Hawthorne, Kate Chopin, and Edith Wharton's experience of Europe.

The life-wonderers, the adventurers of Wharton's novels, are the female intruders. Like Wharton, they are outsiders, outcasts faced with hostility and intolerance and repressiveness. Like Wharton they rebel, often only to be punished for their rebellion, but sometimes to find freedom and joy. Only the intruders in Wharton's fiction can live up to her own criterion for survival: "In spite of illness, in spite even of the arch-enemy sorrow, one *can* remain alive . . . if one is unafraid of change, insatiable in intellectual curiosity, interested in big things, and happy in small ways." Their vitality, their spontaneity, their very *aliveness* in the midst of a world designed to stifle that spirit, make the intruders Wharton's spiritual kin, reflectors of the conflicts and triumphs of her own life.

Excerpted from Carol Wershoven, *The Female Intruder in the Novels of Edith Wharton* (Cranbury, NJ: Associated University Presses, 1982). Reprinted by permission of the publisher. (Endnotes and in-text page references to *Ethan Frome* in the original have been omitted in this reprint.)

Wharton the aristocratic New Yorker is a sister not only to the intruders of her own class, like Ellen Olenska [a character in *The Age of Innocence*] or to people of her own profession, like the writer Margaret Aubyn [a character in *The Touchstone*], but to the heroines of all types and classes who fill her novels. In fact, the heroine of the novel that presents the pattern of the intruder in its simplest, barest form is about as far removed from Edith Wharton in class as she can be. This intruder is Mattie Silver, the farm drudge of *Ethan Frome*, a woman who, superficially, is different from Wharton herself and from other more intelligent, more socially polished intruders.

MATTIE AS A TYPICAL WHARTON CHARACTER

And yet Mattie's story, and *Ethan Frome*, present the struggle of the intruder in society in almost parable form. There is the typical setting of the prison world—here Starkfield, a place of desolation, of living death. It is a town of eternal winter, for in it nothing changes, nothing develops or grows. Images of death and stasis crowd this novel; in the countryside the occasional farmhouse stands isolated, "mute and cold as a gravestone," and the very tombstones seem to call out mockingly to the passerby: "We never got away—how should you?" Starkfield's chief prisoner is Ethan Frome, the typical Wharton male, a man of greater perception and sensitivity than those around him, trapped by his weakness and by marriage to Zeena, a living symbol of Starkfield and its paralysis.

When Mattie Silver enters this world she disrupts it, changing the lives of Ethan and Zeena forever. She is at once contrasted with the conventional Zeena, her vitality and gaiety introduced in the first description of her, dancing, flushed by a warm fire, her red "fascinator" streaming behind her as Ethan watches her outside, in darkness and snow. Juxtaposed with this scene is the reader's first glimpse of Zeena, a grim specter at the threshold of her home,

> tall and angular, one hand drawing a quilted counterpane to her flat breast, while the other held a lamp. The light . . . drew out of the darkness her puckered throat and the projecting wrist of the hand that clutched the quilt, and deepened fantastically the hollows and prominence of her high-boned face under its ring of crimping pins.

Mattie brings Ethan back to life, and soon "all his life was lived in the sight and sound of Mattie Silver, and he could no longer conceive of its being otherwise." Her presence is like "the lighting of a fire on a cold hearth," and her energy revitalizes the despairing Ethan: "from the first," Mattie, "the quicker, finer, more expressive, instead of crushing him by the contrast, had given him something of her own ease and freedom."

When society, in the form of the silent and vicious Zeena, expels the intruder, Ethan is offered a chance to escape from Starkfield himself. But, again like the typical Wharton male, Ethan cannot free himself, for he has never left his winter world except in fantasy. Ethan has never acted or planned to make his fantasies real, but instead has only imagined "we'll always go on living here together. . . . He was never so happy with her as when he abandoned himself to these dreams." In the real world Ethan remains a prisoner of society.

It is Mattie who must take the initiative, who must make one last attempt to keep Ethan and to free him in the only way she can think of—in death. Mattie suggests the attempt, willing her lover down the hill, encouraging, pushing, forcing him to take the only way out. But the escape through

---

WHAT MATTIE MEANS TO ETHAN

In this excerpt from Ethan Frome, *Ethan watches Mattie dancing while he waits outside in the snow, and he thinks of the new lease on life her youthful happiness and optimism have given him.*

Mattie Silver had lived under his roof for a year, and from early morning till they met at supper he had frequent chances of seeing her; but no moments in her company were comparable to those when, her arm in his, and her light step flying to keep time with his long stride, they walked back through the night to the farm. He had taken to the girl from the first day, when he had driven over to the Flats to meet her, and she had smiled and waved to him from the train, crying out, "You must be Ethan!" as she jumped down with her bundles, while he reflected, looking over her slight person: "She don't look much on housework, but she ain't a fretter, anyhow." But it was not only that the coming to his house of a bit of hopeful young life was like the lighting of a fire on a cold hearth. The girl was more than the bright serviceable creature he had thought her. She had an eye to see and an ear to hear: he could show her things and tell her things, and taste the bliss of feeling that all he imparted left long reverberations and echoes he could wake at will.

death is denied the pair, for as Ethan is about to hit the fatal tree, the real world intrudes: "his wife's face, with twisted monstrous lineaments, thrust itself between him and his goal." Starkfield has won. It has gained a new prisoner for its frozen world. The novel ends as it began, with paralysis; not only Mattie's physical paralysis, but the living death that results when one cannot change, cannot act. Mattie's fate is the worst of all the Wharton intruders, for although others die in their attempts to widen their worlds, Mattie, more horribly, lives. Crippled, querulous, damned, she is transformed into the proper inhabitant of Starkfield.

Mattie as an Atypical Wharton Character

Ethan Frome is the bleakest and perhaps the cruelest of Wharton's novels. It contains no prettiness of scene nor polish of manners to soften the impact and consequences of the intrusion of its heroine into the nightmare world of Starkfield. Its intruder herself, Mattie, lacks the wit and critical intelligence of many other Wharton intruders. And yet the book is the archetypal Wharton novel; the story, however remote from New York and disguised by its bareness, is the archetypal Wharton conflict.

It is the essential conflict, the recurring motif, of the woman who is at once more vital, braver, and more receptive to all of life than the society she must confront and challenge. . . . In the essential qualities of courage and energy, in her role as disrupter and as living alternative to the suffocation around her, Mattie is an intruder. Perhaps Mattie and Starkfield are deliberately different from other Wharton heroines and other Wharton settings, are disguised and remote from Wharton's own milieu, because what happens to Mattie represents Wharton's hidden fear: the fear that there is no escape from stifling convention, that the brave life-wonderer will only be destroyed.

CHAPTER 4

The Case for and Against *Ethan Frome*

READINGS ON
ETHAN FROME

"A Dead Book": The Novel's Tragic Story Remains Flawed

Lionel Trilling

In this famous reading of *Ethan Frome*, Lionel Trilling criticizes the novel on moral grounds. Edith Wharton does not create a larger context within which this tragedy can occur and through which the reader might be instructed. Trilling claims, for example, that tragic Shakespearean figures such as Macbeth and King Lear are rendered prone to the destructive power of ambition and overweening pride. Their final realization of how these flaws have destroyed both themselves and those they love moves the reader beyond the characters' words and actions and into the moral purpose behind their having been created. The suffering of Ethan and Mattie, on the other hand, exists only in and of itself. Thus, the work fails to move beyond a cold exercise, and for Trilling, it lacks any deeper warmth and humanity. Lionel Trilling taught at Columbia University for many years and wrote a number of classic studies of English and American literature and culture, including *Sincerity and Authenticity* (1972), *Beyond Culture* (1965), and *The Liberal Imagination* (1950).

We can never speak of Edith Wharton without some degree of respect. She brought to her novels a strong if limited intelligence, and notable powers of observation, and a genuine desire to tell the truth, a desire which in some parts she satisfied. But she was a woman in whom we cannot fail to see a limitation of heart, and this limitation makes itself manifest as a literary and moral deficiency of her work, and of *Ethan Frome* especially. It appears in the deadness of her

Excerpted from Lionel Trilling, "The Morality of Inertia," in *Great Moral Dilemmas*, edited by Robert MacIver (New York: Harper and Row, 1956). Copyright © 1956 by Lionel Trilling. Reprinted with the permission of The Wylie Agency, Inc.

prose, and more flagrantly in the suffering of her characters. When the characters of a story suffer, they do so at the behest of their author—the author is responsible for their suffering and must justify his cruelty by the seriousness of his moral intention. The author of *Ethan Frome*, it seemed to me, could not lay claim to any such justification. Her intention in writing the story was not adequate to the dreadful fate she contrives for her characters. She but indulges herself by what she contrives—she is, as the phrase goes, "merely literary." This is not to say that the merely literary intention does not make its very considerable effects. There is in *Ethan Frome* an image of life-in-death, of hell-on-earth, which is not easily to be forgotten: the crippled Ethan, and Zeena, his dreadful wife, and Mattie, the once charming girl he had loved, now bedridden and querulous with pain, all living out their death in the kitchen of the desolate Frome farm—a perpetuity of suffering memorializes a moment of passion. It is terrible to contemplate, it is unforgettable, but the mind can do nothing with it, can only endure it.

My new reading of the book, then, did not lead me to suppose that it justified its reputation, but only confirmed my recollection that *Ethan Frome* was a dead book, the product of mere will, of the cold hard literary will. What is more, it seemed to me quite unavailable to any moral discourse. In the context of morality, there is nothing to say about *Ethan Frome*. It presents no moral issue at all.

For consider the story it tells. A young man of good and gentle character is the only son of a New England farm couple. He has some intellectual gifts and some desire to know the world, and for a year he is happy attending a technical school in a nearby city. But his father is incapacitated by a farm accident, and Ethan dutifully returns to manage the failing farm and sawmill. His father dies; his mother loses her mental faculties, and during her last illness she is nursed by a female relative whom young Ethan marries, for no reason other than that he is bemused by loneliness. The new wife immediately becomes a shrew, a harridan, and a valetudinarian—she lives only to be ill. Because Zeena now must spare herself, the Fromes take into their home a gentle and charming young girl, a destitute cousin of the wife. Ethan and Mattie fall in love, innocently but deeply. The wife, perceiving this, plans to send the girl away, her place to be taken by a hired servant whose wages the husband cannot possibly afford. In despair at their separation Mattie and Ethan attempt suicide. They mean to die by sledding down a steep hill and crashing into a great elm at the bottom. Their plan fails: both survive the crash, Ethan to be sorely crippled, Mattie to be bedridden in perpetual pain. Now the wife Zeena surrenders her claim to a mysterious pathology and becomes the devoted nurse and jailer of the lovers. The terrible tableau to which I have referred is ready for our inspection.

It seemed to me that it was quite impossible to talk about this story. This is not to say that the story is without interest as a story, but what interest it may have does not yield discourse, or at least not moral discourse. . . .

WHAT IS TRUE TRAGEDY?

It is, as I have suggested, a very great fault in *Ethan Frome* that it presents no moral issue, and no moral reverberation. A certain propriety controls the literary representation of human suffering. This propriety dictates that the representation of pain may not be, as it were, gratuitous; it must not be an end in itself. The naked act of representing, or contemplating, human suffering is a self-indulgence, and it may be a cruelty. Between a tragedy and a spectacle in the Roman circus there is at least this much similarity, that the pleasure both afford derives from observing the pain of others. A tragedy is always on the verge of cruelty. What saves it from the actuality of cruelty is that it has an intention beyond itself. This intention may be so simple a one as that of getting us to do something practical about the cause of the suffering or to help actual sufferers, or at least to feel that we should; or it may lead us to look beyond apparent causes to those which the author wishes us to think of as more real, such as Fate, or the will of the gods, or the will of God; or it may challenge our fortitude or intelligence or piety.

A sense of the necessity of some such intention animates all considerations of the strange paradox of tragedy. Aristotle is concerned to solve the riddle of how the contemplation of human suffering can possibly be pleasurable, of why its pleasure is permissible. He wanted to know what literary conditions were needed to keep a tragedy from being a mere display of horror. Here it is well to remember that the Greeks were not so concerned as we have been led to believe to keep all dreadful things off the stage—in the presentation of Aris-

totle's favorite tragedy, [Sophocles' *Oedipus the King*,] the audience saw [Oedipus's mother-wife] Jocasta hanging from a
beam, it saw the representation of Oedipus's bloody sightless
eye sockets. And so, Aristotle discovered, or pretended to discover, that tragedy did certain things to protect itself from
being merely cruel. It chose, Aristotle said, a certain kind of
hero; he was of a certain social and moral stature; he had a
certain degree of possibility of free choice, or at least the appearance or illusion of free choice; he must justify his fate,
or seem to justify it, by his moral condition, being neither
wholly good nor wholly bad, having a particular fault that
collaborates with destiny to bring about his ruin. The purpose of all these specifications for the tragic hero is to assure
us that we witness something more than mere passivity
when we witness the hero's suffering, that we witness something more than suffering, that the suffering has, as we say,
some meaning, some show of rationality.

Aristotle's theory of tragedy has had its way with the
world to an extent which is perhaps out of proportion to its
comprehensiveness and accuracy. Its success is largely due
to, its having dealt so openly with the paradox of tragedy. It
serves to explain away any guilty feelings that we may have
at deriving pleasure from suffering.

But at the same time that the world has accepted Aristotle's theory of tragedy, it has also been a little uneasy about
some of its implications. The element of the theory that
causes uneasiness in modern times is the matter of the
stature of the hero. To a society touched by egalitarian sentiments, the requirement that the hero be a man of rank
seems to deny the presumed dignity of tragedy to men of
lesser status. And to a culture which questions the freedom
of the will, Aristotle's hero seems to be a little beside the
point. Aristotle's prescription for the tragic hero is clearly
connected with his definition, in his *Ethics*, of the nature of
an ethical action. He tells us that a truly ethical action must
be a free choice between two alternatives. This definition is
then wonderfully complicated by a further requirement—
that the moral man must be so trained in making the right
choice that he makes it as a matter of habit, makes it, as it
were, instinctively. Yet it *is* a choice, and reason plays a part
in its making. But we, of course, don't give to reason the
same place in the moral life that Aristotle gave it. And in general, over the past hundred and fifty years, dramatists and

novelists have tried their hand at the representation of human suffering without the particular safeguards against cruelty which Aristotle perceived, or contrived. A very large part of the literature of Western Europe may be understood in terms of an attempt to invert or criticize the heroic prescription of the hero, by burlesque and comedy, or by the insistence on the commonplace, the lowering of the hero's social status and the diminution of his power of reasoned choice. . . .

THE MORAL FAILURE OF *ETHAN FROME*

Edith Wharton was following where others led. Her impulse in conceiving the story of Ethan Frome was not, however, that of moral experimentation. It was, as I have said, a purely literary impulse, in the bad sense of the word literary. Her aim is not that of [William] Wordsworth in any of his stories of the suffering poor, to require it of us that we open our minds to realization of the kinds of people whom suffering touches. Nor is it that of [Gustave] Flaubert in *Madame Bovary*, to wring from sordid circumstances all the pity and terror of an ancient tragic fable. Nor is it that of [Charles] Dickens or [Emile] Zola, to shake us with the perception of social injustice, to instruct us in the true nature of social life and to dispose us to indignant opinion and action. These are not essentially literary intentions; they are moral intentions. But all that Edith Wharton has in mind is to achieve that grim tableau of which I have spoken, of pain and imprisonment, of life-in-death. About the events that lead up to this tableau, there is nothing she finds to say, nothing whatever. The best we can say about the meaning of the story is that it might perhaps be a subject of discourse in the context of rural sociology—it might be understood to exemplify the thesis that love and joy do not flourish on poverty stricken New England farms. If we try to bring it into the context of morality, its meaning is limited to mere cultural considerations—that is, to people who like their literature to show the "smiling aspects of life," it may be thought to say, "This is the aspect that life really has, as grim as this"; while to people who repudiate a literature that represents only the smiling aspects of life it says, "How intelligent and how brave you are to be able to understand that life is as grim as this." It is really not very much to say.

And yet there is in *Ethan Frome* an idea of very consider-

A WORK OF UNBEARABLE TRAGEDY

The review of Ethan Frome *published in the* New York Times Book Review *praises the power and skill of the work while maintaining that it lacks compassion.*

Wharton prefers to present life in its unsmiling aspects, to look at it with the eye of the tragic poet, not with the deep sympathy, smiling tenderness, and affectionate tolerance of the greatest novelists. Thus she never shows life as it is, as the great novelists do, but as an aspect or view of life—the reflex of life on the writer if you will—which colors all things with some mastering mood of him or her.

The present grim tale of a bud of romance ice-bound and turned into a frozen horror in the frigid setting of a New England Winter landscape is conceived in the remorseless spirit of the Greek tragic muse. The rigidity of the bleak Puritan outlook on life does duty for the relentless Fates. It is a powerful and skillful performance and seems to recreate a life and an atmosphere essentially the same as that which breathes in the romances of [Nathaniel] Hawthorne. That atmosphere is, no doubt, the true emanation of the soul of New England—that New England, warped by the dour theology of the cruel and fanatic age that planted it, which was Hawthorne's own, and which now has retired to such frozen fastnesses as the lonely and starved village among the barren hills in which Wharton places her story. . . .

It is a cruel story. It is a compelling and haunting story. But it is a story which a bald telling, without the art which has thrown the crude material of the plot into due dramatic perspective and given it poetic atmosphere, could easily make absurd, or even revolting. The mere saying that Wharton has brought about the catastrophe by sending two of her principal characters coasting down an icy hill and "smashing them up" for life—but not killing them—against a great tree near the bottom, conveys an impression of clumsiness and brutality which only the actual reading of the story will avail to dispel. Wharton has, in fact, chosen to build of small, crude things and a rude and violent event a structure whose purpose is the infinite refinement of torture. All that is human and pitiful and tender in the tale—and there is much—is designed and contrived to sharpen the keen edge of that torture. And the victims lie stretched upon the rack for twenty years.

"Three Lives in Supreme Torture," *New York Times Book Review,* October 8, 1911.

able importance. It is there by reason of the author's deficiencies, not by reason of her powers—it is there because it suits Edith Wharton's rather dull literary intention to be content with telling a story about people who do not make moral decisions, whose fate cannot have moral reverberations. The idea is this: that moral inertia, the *not* making of moral decisions, constitutes a very large part of the moral life of humanity.

This isn't an idea that literature likes to deal with. Literature is charmed by energy and dislikes inertia. It characteristically represents morality as positive action. The same is true of the moral philosophy of the West—has been true ever since Aristotle defined a truly moral act by its energy of reason, of choice. A later development of this tendency said that an act was really moral only if it went against the inclination of the person performing the act: the idea was parodied as saying that one could not possibly act morally to one's friends, only to one's enemies.

Yet the dull daily world sees something below this delightful preoccupation of literature and moral philosophy. It is aware of the morality of inertia, and of its function as a social base, as a social cement. It knows that duties are done for no other reason than that they are said to be duties; for no other reason, sometimes, than that the doer has not really been able to conceive of any other course, has, perhaps, been afraid to think of any other course.... How often the moral act is performed not because we are we but because we are there! This is the morality of habit, or the morality of biology. This is Ethan Frome's morality, simple, unquestioning, passive, even masochistic. His duties as a son are discharged because he is a son; his duties as a husband are discharged because he is a husband. He does nothing because he is a moral man. At one point in his story he is brought to moral crisis—he must choose between his habituated duty to his wife and his duty and inclination to the girl he loves. It is quite impossible for him to deal with the dilemma in the high way that literature and moral philosophy prescribe, by reason and choice. Choice is incompatible with his idea of his existence; he can only elect to die.

Literature, of course, is not wholly indifferent to what I have called the morality of habit and biology, the morality of inertia. But literature, when it deals with this morality, is tempted to qualify its dullness by endowing it with a certain high grace. There is never any real moral choice for the Felicité of Flaubert's story, "A Simple Heart." She is all pious habit of virtue, and of blind, unthinking, unquestioning love. There are, of course, actually such people as Felicité, simple, good, loving—quite stupid in their love, not choosing where to bestow it. We meet such people frequently in literature. . . . They are of a quite different order of being from those who try the world with their passion and their reason; they are by way of being saints, of the less complicated kind. They do not really exemplify what I meant by the morality of inertia or of biology. Literature is uncomfortable in the representation of the morality of inertia or of biology, and overcomes its discomfort by representing it with the added grace of that extravagance which we denominate saintliness.

But the morality of inertia is to be found in precise exemplification in one of Wordsworth's poems. Wordsworth is preeminent among the writers who experimented in the representation of new kinds and bases of moral action—he has a genius for imputing moral existence to people who, according to the classical morality, should have no life at all. And he has the coldness to make this imputation without at the same time imputing the special grace and interest of saintliness. The poem I have in mind is ostensibly about a flower, but the transition from the symbol to the human fact is clearly, if awkwardly, made. The flower is a small celandine, and the poet observes that it has not, in the natural way of flowers, folded itself against rough weather:

But lately, one rough day, this Flower I passed
And recognized it, though in altered form,
Now standing as an offering to the blast,
And buffeted at will by rain and storm.

I stopped, and said with inly-muttered voice,
It doth not love the shower nor seek the cold;
This neither is its courage nor its choice,
But its necessity in being old.

Neither courage nor choice, but necessity: it cannot do otherwise. Yet it acts as if by courage and choice. This is the morality imposed by brute circumstance, by biology, by habit, by the unspoken social demand which we have not the strength to refuse, or, often, to imagine refusing. People are scarcely ever praised for living according to this morality—we do not suppose it to be a morality at all until we see it being broken.

This is morality as it is conceived by the great mass of

people in the world. And with this conception of morality goes the almost entire negation of any connection between morality and destiny. A superstitious belief in retribution may play its part in the thought of simple people, but essentially they think of catastrophes as fortuitous, without explanation, without reason. They live in the moral universe of the *Book of Job.* In complex lives, morality does in some part determine destiny; in most lives it does not. Between the moral life of Ethan and Mattie and their terrible fate we cannot make any reasonable connection. Only a moral judgment cruel to the point of insanity could speak of it as anything but accidental.

Ethan Frome: A Truly Tragic Novel

Geoffrey Walton

Wharton critic Geoffrey Walton even-handedly examines the artistic merit of *Ethan Frome.* Walton concludes by guardedly praising the novel, mostly because it gives noble passions and a tragic dimension to a kind of people to whom writers do not usually ascribe tragedy.

It is not surprising that *Ethan Frome* has been overpraised, though it is strange that it has caught more attention than [Wharton's 1917 novel] *Summer.* Edith Wharton has told us about the early draft in French and about her joy in producing the final version under [her friend] Walter Berry's exacting scrutiny:

> For years I had wanted to draw life as it really was in the derelict mountain villages of New England, a life even in my time, and a thousandfold more a generation earlier, utterly unlike that seen through the rose-coloured spectacles of my predecessors, Mary Wilkins and Sarah Orne Jewett. In those days, the snow-bound villages of Western Massachusetts were still grim places, morally and physically: insanity, incest and slow mental and moral starvation were hidden away behind the paintless wooden house-fronts of the long village street, or in the isolated farm-houses on the neighbouring hills; and Emily Brontë would have found as savage tragedies in our remoter valleys as on her Yorkshire moors.

The story is especially closely written, the narrator being made to assume the role of editor; he says he coordinates, which is perhaps a better expression, as he produces a continuous story and not a collection of anecdotes, which might at first sight have been more naturalistic; Edith Wharton had, however, carefully thought out reasons in terms of both subject and story-telling technique for using the method she borrowed from [Honoré] Balzac's *La Grande Bretêche.*

Excerpted from Geoffrey Walton, *Edith Wharton: A Critical Interpretation* (Cranbury, NJ: Associated University Presses, 1970). Reprinted by permission of the publisher.

Within his role, the narrator is the omniscient author; he interprets what he has been told; no one could have told him some of the details that he puts into his "vision." The name Starkfield is all too suitable for the remote Massachusetts village, and the landscape is as carefully chosen as any of [novelist Thomas] Hardy's. One is not made strongly aware of the religious background as a body of doctrine but one has a sense of a narrow world, whose foundations are religious, closing in on the inhabitants and of poverty, sickness, and inescapable unhappiness. Only little breakaways at rare intervals are possible; it is appropriate to the place as well as to Puritan tradition that Endurance [Frome] has been a women's name. The opening sentence sets the tone; it is informal, businesslike, and utterly detached:

> I had the story, bit by bit, from various people, and, as generally happens in such cases, each time it was a different story.

The implication is, as Edith Wharton wished to suggest, of rural inarticulateness and exasperating inconsequence, which the narrator has ordered and disciplined. One is then confronted with Frome, "the ruin of a man," crippled by an accident, and one infers the existence of a hypochondriac wife; "'. . . he's been in Starkfield too many winters. . . . Most of the smart ones get away.'" sums up the two basic features of the scene and its influence, the numbing rather than bracing cold and the difficulty of communications. Frome, however, is not a clod; he preserves an interest in science from early days at a Technical College. When at the climax of the introductory section the narrator is snowbound at the Frome farm, even the house looks appropriately "stunted" because Frome has pulled down the wing linking it to the farm buildings which, it is said, "seem[s] to be the centre, the actual hearthstone, of a New England farm." The impression that everything has been contrived and the impression of spontaneous happening are just about equally strong, and the plan of the book as a whole, with its carefully arranged flashbacks, accentuates both this more literary quality in a narrow sense and also the essential fatalism. It is a tale of gratuitous and unavoidable frustration of natural impulses, of revolt, and of suffering. There is again no social conflict; human and inanimate environment seem all one. We already know that Ethan Frome has married the cousin who nursed his senile mother. We learn later that Zeena was once a "smart" and lively bride, but she has become both the

supreme product and, for Frome, the ever-present representative of that environment, a silent brooding power from
which he cannot escape. She represents no one particular
oppression, such as Puritan tradition, but the whole range of
suspicions, obligations, and restrictions, large and small,
that arise in an isolated and impoverished community, stiff-
ened by Calvinism. There is a decided element of caricature

A VERY HUMAN TRAGEDY

A reviewer from Bookman *sees in the grand inevitability of*
Ethan Frome *all the elements of a great tragedy.*

Wharton has more than satisfied one's expectation, and her art
has never been shown to greater advantage than in this story of
Ethan Frome, the young Massachusetts farmer. It is a tragedy,
almost unendurably poignant, but justified by its inevitable-
ness. From his youth Fate dealt hardly with Ethan. His father
died, leaving him a bleak unproductive farm, and a failing saw-
mill. After a lingering illness, his mother also died. That was in
the Fall; had it been in the Spring his future might have been
different, but Ethan dared not face the winter alone in this
"New England farmhouse that made the landscape lonelier."
Then he took his first step toward the abyss: he asked Zeena,
the tall, uncomely, raw-boned woman who had nursed his
mother, to be his wife. From that time his life was a martyrdom, for Zeena soon showed her real character as a sickly,
querulous neurotic. Then came the next stroke of Destiny. To
save expense, for the poverty at the farm was grinding, Mattie
Silver, the penniless young cousin of Zeena, was invited to live
with them. As the girl served without pay her cousin suggested
that on the rare occasions, when there was an entertainment in
the village, Mattie should go to it, so that she should not feel too
sharp a contrast between the life she had left and the isolation
of the farm. On these occasions, Ethan, although at first he had
inwardly demurred at the extra toil imposed on him, was accustomed to fetch home his wife's cousin. Soon he found himself wishing that the village might give all its nights to revelry.
Gradually the wife's suspicions are aroused; a hired girl is employed, and Mattie must go. Poverty makes Ethan helpless;
money might have saved two lives, if not three, but there is
none. So the blow falls in the last act that is to consign the three
to a living death. It is a beautiful, sad, but intensely human
story, working out to its final conclusion with all the inevitability of a great Greek tragedy.

"Inevitability of a Great Greek Tragedy," *Bookman,* January 1912.

in the treatment of Zeena. With "her hard perpendicular
bonnet" and the "querulous lines from her thin nose to the
corners of her mouth," she appears as the very incarnation
of dyspepsia and uncharitableness. We are shown Frome
torn between the exacting dominance of this presence and
his natural attraction to Mattie Silver, *her* young and destitute cousin—Mattie's story is all of a piece with the rest—
who has been brought to help in the house. This domestic
situation is cunningly but effectively sandwiched into an account of Ethan Frome fetching the girl back from a dance;
the contrast brings out his emotional situation with simple
forcefulness. References to Mattie's incompetence and her
vague intellectual sympathy add to the sum of "tempta-
tions," which are so inevitable that they seem merely part of
his fatal environment; circumstances, action, sensation, and
wishful thinking are clearly and naturally related in the description of their return home:

> For the first time he stole his arm about her, and she did not
> resist. They walked on as if they were floating on a summer
> stream.

> Zeena always went to bed as soon as she had had her supper,
> and the shutterless windows of the house were dark. A dead
> cucumber-vine dangled from the porch like the crape
> streamer died to the door for a death, and the thought flashed
> through Ethan's brain: "If it was there for Zeena—" Then he
> had a distinct sight of his wife lying in their bedroom asleep,
> her mouth slightly open, her false teeth in a tumbler by the
> bed.

When, between the presentation of this situation and the
consequence, Ethan Frome and Mattie are thrown together,
he is totally inhibited by his opportunity, but a trivial accident results in Mattie's departure in favor of a "hired girl,"
which implies financial ruin as well as emotional stagnation
for Frome. Zeena's state is summed up with a grimly comic
reference and an ominous suggestion:

> Almost everybody in the neighbourhood had "troubles,"
> frankly localized and specified; but only the chosen had
> "complications." To have them was in itself a distinction,
> though it was also, in most cases, a death-warrant.

IS THE NOVEL'S ENDING OVERLY CONTRIVED?

Each succeeding episode increases the feeling of inevitability,
and images of small disasters, such as "netted butterflies," in-
crease the pathos. Frome forms wild plans for escaping West

with Mattie, until he realizes that he cannot even afford the fare, and he runs through a gamut of impulses, including deceit of friends; it is all too primitive to be called social rebellion. Though the final act is described as "some erratic impulse," one feels that it is the last of a sequence. The last "coast" down the frozen hill and the suicide pact that fails are a symbolic culmination, very powerfully rendered, of the main theme of head-on frustration. The image of Zeena, obtruded in Frome's consciousness just before the crash, reminds us of the theme of infidelity. This is a minor element, however; there has been no real moral any more than social conflict. Ethan Frome's actions are the product of his environment and his natural temperament and the author does not blame him; Zeena calls Mattie "a bad girl" for breaking a plate, but the moral overtone, though implied, is not very important. One "accident" partly helps them; the next, their survival, is disastrous.

The epilogue presents a state of death in life and life in death, the two cripples looked after by the ex-hypochondriac in a setting of direst poverty; Zeena has developed thus far morally. One of the narrator's informants, a character comparable to Nellie Dean, [the narrator of Emily Brontë's novel *Wuthering Heights*,] registers the grimness and the pathos and Frome's surviving pride. There is no suggestion of either punishment or release, simply of continuous pain.

OVERVIEW AND RETROSPECTIVE ASSESSMENT

It is not difficult to criticize *Ethan Frome.* Despite, indeed perhaps because of, Edith Wharton's skill, one feels it is a little too inevitable. The contrasts are a little too sharp, the setting a little too bleak, the characters almost caricature—of a grim kind, the disaster melodramatic, and the end unrelievedly wretched. Apart from the formal derivation from Balzac, the construction and the atmosphere in fact remind one more of Hardy than of Emily Brontë; the book lacks both the delicacy and the power of *Wuthering Heights.* One sees a certain kinship between Frome with his thwarted intellectual ambition and Jude Fawley. It is a peasant tragedy in an American setting. Ultimately one probably agrees with [critic Lionel] Trilling's criticism, but one must recognize the distinction of the story, as he recognizes the stoic virtues it offers for our admiration, the endurance and self-respect in the face of hopeless odds. . . . Insofar as he rebels, Ethan

Frome seems to rebel against life itself—as it exists at Stark-field—rather than against vestigial Puritanism or the social system, but his self-respect and independence, preserved at any cost, are fundamental middle-class qualities.... Tragedy culminates in an all-out assault on these values, the last refuge of the individual, and, limited as the scope of it, one feels the ultimate human significance of what is involved in the particular and the class situation.... Ethan Frome keeps his economic independence..., but in conditions that almost nullify it. Edith Wharton has recorded certain social facts, the resignation and pathetic conservatism, the personal pride and desperate individualism of a large number of people of a certain type and class background. She invites us to admire, but to realize the misery to which devotion to these values may lead. Her picture does not fit into any version of the class struggle except as an embarrassing problem, but one should be grateful to her for showing it, as one is to her for showing that tragedy is possible also among the merely well-to-do.

CHRONOLOGY

1862

Born Edith Newbold Jones on January 24 in New York City, the only daughter of George Frederick and Lucretia Rhinelander Jones; sister to Harry and Freddie Jones. Edith is born into a life of wealth and privilege, her family being a part of the most exclusive segment of New York society.

1866–1872

Due to the post–Civil War economic depression and subsequent fall in income, the family moves to Europe to economize, living in France, Italy, and Germany.

1872

Family returns to America, and for the next eight years Edith lives in New York City and spends summers in Newport, Rhode Island.

1877–1880

Writes an unpublished novella, *Fast and Loose* (1877); has a collection of her poetry, *Verses*, published privately; and poems appear in the *Atlantic Monthly* (1880).

1880

Meets and becomes engaged to Harry Stevens in Newport; at the end of the year the family moves to the south of France due to her father's failing health; Stevens later joins the family.

1882

Edith's father dies, and she returns to America with her mother; breaks her engagement to Harry Stevens.

1883

Meets Walter Berry, who becomes one of the central figures in her life; also meets her future husband, Edward "Teddy" Robbins Wharton, who is thirteen years older than she.

1885

Marries Teddy Wharton on April 29, and the couple begins a pattern of spending half of the year in America and the other half (February through June) in Europe.

1888

Having received $20,000 after her father's death, Edith inherits an additioinal $120,000 from a cousin on her father's side of the family. This legacy assures her and Teddy's financial security and independence.

1890–1894

Publishes her first short story, "Mrs. Manstey's View" (1890), and publishes three more in *Scribner's;* suffers from a series of physical and mental illnesses that will persist for the rest of the 1890s.

1897

She publishes *The Decoration of Houses* (coauthored with architect Ogden Codman); friendship with Walter Berry begins again after an absence of fourteen years.

1898

Seeks treatment in Philadelphia with famous "rest-cure" physician S. Weir Mitchell after suffering a nervous breakdown.

1899

Publishes her first collection of stories, *The Greater Inclination.*

1900

Publishes *The Touchstone*, a novella, and begins work on her first novel, *The Valley of Decision*, set in eighteenth-century Italy and eventually published in 1902.

1901

Buys and builds on a property in Lenox, Massachusetts, a then-fashionable summer resort in the Berkshire mountains; publishes her second collection of short stories, *Crucial Instances;* Edith's mother dies in Paris.

1902

Begins her friendship with novelist Henry James; *The Valley of Decision* is published and is well received.

1904–1905

Third collection of stories, *The Descent of Man*, is published; her knowledge of Italy, gleaned from extensive travel throughout the country, bears fruit in the form of two books, *Italian Villas and Their Gardens* (1904) and *Italian Backgrounds* (1905); publishes one of her finest novels, *The House of Mirth* (1905), which is a best-seller in America.

1907

Paris becomes the focus of her life in Europe as she rents an apartment on the Rue de Varenne; Edith is now fully engaged socially and intellectually with the literary worlds of both England and France; publishes her third novel, *The Fruit of the Tree.*

1908

Teddy Wharton, feeling increasingly estranged from his wife and the society that has grown around her literary success and fame, begins to suffer serious health problems, including gout and depression; Edith begins a love affair with Morton Fullerton, an American journalist living in Paris.

1909–1910

Edith ends her affair with Fullerton; beginning of estrangement from Teddy Wharton, whose physical problems have increased and whose behavior has become more and more erratic; Edith publishes a volume of poetry and her fifth collection of stories, *Tales of Men and Ghosts.*

1911–1912

Publishes novella *Ethan Frome* (1911), and her first novel in five years, *The Reef* (1912). Begins to negotiate a separation from Teddy, and their home in Massachusetts, the Mount, is sold in June 1912.

1913

Edith's divorce from Teddy is granted on April 16; publishes what she considered one of her finest novels, *The Custom of the Country.*

1914–1918

Lives in Paris during World War I; heavily invests her time and energy in the French and British cause; responsible for feeding, clothing, and establishing shelters for refugees; is made chevalier of the Legion of Honor of France for her war efforts; during the war, she publishes *Fighting France* (1915), a collection of her reports from the front line of the fighting and *Summer* (1917); Henry James dies in February 1916; in 1918 Edith buys Pavillon Colombe outside of Paris; she will divide her time between there and the south of France for the rest of her life.

1920–1921

Publishes in 1920 one of her most successful and best-loved novels, *The Age of Innocence;* the novel is awarded the Pulitzer Prize in 1921.

1922–1923

The Glimpses of the Moon, another best-seller, is published in 1922; follows in 1923 with the less successful *A Son at the Front,* her novel of World War I.

1923

Publishes a collection of four novellas, *Old New York,* and becomes the first woman ever to be awarded the National Institute of Arts and Letters Gold Medal.

1924

Publishes *The Mother's Recompense,* which is considered one of her better late novels, and also a work of criticism, *The Writing of Fiction.*

1926

Is elected to the National Institute of Arts and Letters.

1927–1928

Publishes two more best-selling novels, *Twilight Sleep* and *The Children;* deaths of Walter Berry and Teddy Wharton.

1929

Survives a serious bout of pneumonia and publishes *Hudson River Bracketed;* a stage version of *The Age of Innocence* has a successful run in America.

1931–1932

Elected to the American Academy of Arts and Letters; publishes her last completed novel, *The Gods Arrive,* in 1932.

1934

Publishes her autobiography, *A Backward Glance.*

1936–1938

Publishes her ninth short story collection, *The World Over,* in 1936; suffers a stroke on June 1, 1937, and dies on August 11; her uncompleted novel, *The Buccaneers,* is published in 1938.

FOR FURTHER RESEARCH

Elizabeth Ammons, *Edith Wharton's Argument with America*. Athens: University of Georgia Press, 1980.

Louis Auchincloss, *Edith Wharton*. Minneapolis: University of Minnesota Press, 1961.

Millicent Bell, *Edith Wharton and Henry James: The Story of Their Friendship*. New York: George Braziller, 1965.

Millicent Bell, ed., *The Cambridge Companion to Wharton*. Cambridge, England: Cambridge University Press, 1995.

Alfred Bendixen and Annette Zilversmit, *Edith Wharton: New Critical Essays*. New York: Granada, 1992.

Harold Bloom, ed., *Edith Wharton*. New York: Chelsea House, 1986.

Janet Goodwyn, *Edith Wharton: Traveller in a Land of Letters*. New York: Macmillan, 1990.

David Holbrook, *Edith Wharton and the Unsatisfactory Man*. New York: St. Martin's, 1991.

Irving Howe, ed., *Edith Wharton: A Collection of Critical Essays*. Englewood Cliffs, NJ: Prentice Hall, 1962.

Hellen Killoran, *Edith Wharton: Art and Illusion*. Tuscaloosa: University of Alabama Press, 1996.

Richard H. Lawson, *Edith Wharton*. New York: Frederick Ungar, 1977.

Gary H. Lindberg, *Edith Wharton and the Novel of Manners*. Charlottesville: University Press of Virginia, 1975.

Marilyn Lyde, *Edith Wharton: Convention and Morality in the Work of a Novelist*. Norman: Oklahoma University Press, 1959.

Margaret McDowell, *Edith Wharton*. Boston: Twayne, 1976.

Blake Nevius, *Edith Wharton: A Study of Her Fiction*. Berkeley and Los Angeles: University of California Press, 1953.

Marlene Springer, *Ethan Frome: A Nightmare of Need*. Boston: Twayne, 1993.

Penelope Vita-Finzi, *Edith Wharton and the Art of Fiction*. New York: St. Martin's, 1990.

Candace Waid, *Edith Wharton's Letters from the Underworld: Fictions of Women and Writing.* Chapel Hill: University of North Carolina Press, 1991.

BIOGRAPHICAL AND HISTORICAL WORKS OF INTEREST

Shari Benstock, *No Gifts from Chance: A Biography of Edith Wharton.* New York: Scribner's, 1994.

Eleanor Dwight, *Edith Wharton: An Extraordinary Life.* New York: Harry Abrams, 1994.

Robert L. Heilbroner and Aaron Singer, *The Economic Transformation of America: 1600 to the Present.* Fort Worth: Harcourt Brace College, 1999.

Howard Mumford Jones, *The Age of Energy: Varieties of American Experience, 1865–1914.* New York: Viking, 1971.

R.W.B. Lewis, *Edith Wharton: A Biography.* New York: Harper and Row, 1975.

Percy Lubbock, *Portrait of Edith Wharton.* New York: Appleton-Century, 1947.

Alan Trachtenberg, *The Incorporation of America: Culture and Society in the Gilded Age.* New York: Hill and Wang, 1982.

Cynthia Griffin Wolff, *A Feast of Words: The Triumph of Edith Wharton.* 2nd ed. New York: Addison-Wesley, 1995.

Sarah Bird Wright, *Edith Wharton: A to Z: The Essential Guide to the Life and Work.* New York: Facts On File, 1998.

WORKS BY EDITH WHARTON

Verses. Newport, RI: C.E. Hammett, 1878.

The Decoration of Houses (with Ogden Codman Jr.). New York: Scribner's, 1897.

The Greater Inclination. New York: Scribner's, 1899.

The Touchstone. New York: Scribner's, 1900.

Crucial Instances. New York: Scribner's, 1901.

The Valley of Decision. New York: Scribner's, 1902.

Sanctuary. New York: Scribner's, 1903.

The Descent of Man and Other Stories. New York: Scribner's, 1904.

Italian Villas and Their Gardens. New York: Scribner's, 1904.

Italian Backgrounds. New York: Scribner's, 1905.

The House of Mirth. New York: Scribner's, 1905.

The Fruit of the Tree. New York: Scribner's, 1907.

Madame de Treymes. New York: Scribner's, 1907.

The Hermit and the Wild Woman and Other Stories. New York: Scribner's, 1908.

A Motor-Flight Through France. New York: Scribner's, 1908.

Artemis to Actaeon and Other Verse. New York: Scribner's, 1909.

Tales of Men and Ghosts. New York: Scribner's, 1910.

Ethan Frome. New York: Scribner's, 1911.

The Reef. New York: Scribner's, 1912.

The Custom of the Country. New York: Scribner's, 1913.

Fighting France. New York: Scribner's, 1915.

Xingu and Other Stories. New York: Scribner's, 1916.

Summer. New York: Appleton, 1917.

The Marne. New York: Appleton, 1918.

French Ways and Their Meaning. New York: Appleton, 1919.

In Morocco. New York: Scribner's, 1920.

The Age of Innocence. New York: Appleton, 1920.

A Son at the Front. New York: Scribner's, 1923.

Old New York. New York: Scribner's, 1924.

The Mother's Recompense. New York: Appleton, 1925.

The Writing of Fiction. New York: Scribner's, 1925.

Twelve Poems. London: Medici Society, 1926.

Here and Beyond. New York: Appleton, 1926.

Twilight Sleep. New York: Appleton, 1927.

The Children. New York: Appleton, 1928.

Hudson River Bracketed. New York: Appleton, 1929.

Certain People. New York: Appleton, 1930.

The Gods Arrive. New York: Appleton, 1932.

The Glimpses of the Moon. New York: Appleton, 1932.

Human Nature. New York: Appleton, 1933.

A Backward Glance. New York: Appleton-Century, 1934.

The World Over. New York: Appleton-Century, 1936.

Ghosts. New York: Appleton-Century, 1937.

Fast and Loose and *The Buccaneers* (ed. Viola Hopkins Winner). Charlottesville: University of Virginia Press, 1993.

INDEX